fishin', fightin', feedin' & farmin'

Jack Hudson

**FREE RIVER PRESS
FOLK LITERATURE SERIES**

Robert Wolf, General Editor

fishin', fightin', feedin' & farmin'

The Life and Times of a West Tennessee Farmer

by Jack Hudson

FREE RIVER PRESS
1208 FRENCH CREEK DRIVE
LANSING, IOWA 52151

ISBN # 1-878781-21-9
© 2000 by Jack Hudson

Free River Press
1208 French Creek Drive
Lansing, Iowa 52151

DEDICATION

to Celia Weakley Hudson
my wife of 63 years

CONTENTS

INTRODUCTION

Jack Hudson is one of the natural born story tellers we so seldom see these days. In a world of increasingly bland yet frenzied people obsessed with counting the grams of fat in their food and the daily fluctuations of the stock market, with Prosaic and e-commerce, Mr. Hudson reminds us that not so long ago people had honest work to do. What Paul Goodman in *Growing Up Absurd* called manly work. Much of it was physical labor.

Labor bred a less self-absorbed personality. And a laboring society living on the land knew from hard experience that Nature can't be clubbed into obedience or outsmarted. One of the greatest modern delusions is that the world will be improved with the elimination of labor, that the curse of Adam can be lifted without perilous consequences to ourselves. Believing this fantasy we have followed the path of increased mechanization, and one of the obvious consequences has been a growing ignorance of our limits. With this loss of self-knowledge, we cannot see that millions of citizens of the most prosperous country on earth are losing character and personality.

Another delusion cherished by moderns is the belief that they are individually self-sufficient. This is reflected in a society which is composed, by and large, of competitive and aggressive individuals. Under such a condition, community becomes an impossibility, and we mourn its loss. We have so few genuine connections with others that we imagine that a cyberspace chatroom forms a community. Lost inside our pressed board boxes called homes, we entertain ourselves by staring at our television and computer screens. Rural America of seventy years ago was a world where entertainment was what you or your neighbors made together. Mutual interdependence of a village formed the basis of community. But now that the cotton for my shirts is grown in one country, the cloth woven in another, and the parts sewn in a third, I have no sense of the shirt as a human artifact. The food for my noon meal is grown on three continents and processed on a fourth. Like the shirt, it is simply a commodity, not a product or symbol

1

of human interaction. I am dependent now on the structure of a system whose parts are expendable. The members of a backwater community are not expendable. Those black and white tenant farmers near RoEllen, Tennessee whom Mr. Hudson describes, enabled each other to weather tough times.

Born into a culture far different from the urban-based, contemporary global culture that is uprooting everything opposed to it, Mr. Hudson has written an important work that gives a vision of how life can be lived. He describes an interracial community where integrity, hard work, and decency are valued above all other traits. It is a brave vision and a noble book.

Mr. Hudson's idiosyncratic spellings and grammar have, for the most part, been left intact, for I agree with English writer Havelock Ellis that obsession with consistency of spelling and syntax is a sign of a language's decline. Better to retain our experience and vision in our own words and syntax than to flatten and homogenize them in a processor.

Robert Wolf

PART I

"WATCH THAT GOAT!"

Granddad, Granny
and Dan the Bulldog

Jack, Frank (father), Bill
(brother), and Gene (nephew)

Celia and Jack
Easter, 1939

4

Granddad and the Model T

When I was 10 my Granddad bought a new 1927 T Model Ford. He was hard of hearing you had to holler for him to hear you.

Everyone was gone one day and my Granddad thought it a good time to learn to drive. Dill and I were playing marbles in the yard when he called us in the house. He wanted to know if I knew how to drive the car. We all went down to the barn. I put the brake on and put the car in neutral. I turned on the key and Dill cranked the car. It was a touring car with a running board you could stand on. I put it in reverse and backed it into the middle of the lott. I got out of the car and stood on the running board next to Granddad. I told him to pull the throttle down just a little. I guess he didn't hear me, he pulled the throttle down all the way. The Ford took one big lunge down the hill. I jumped off the running board the goats went one way, the chickens one way, the horses another way and the car went down the hill into the fence. Dill and I went down and cut the ignition off. Granddad crawled out of the car he was kinda shook up but he was not hurt. The first thing he said was "Why didn't you tell me how to stop it?" I said "You pulled the throttle too far down. I didn't have time to tell you."

Granddad Liked to Fish

My Granddad liked to fish, had rather fish than eat. When he was going by himself he would ride a little roan mare. But when Dill and I were going with him he would hitch the mare to a one horse wagon. Dill and I would bring some hay for her to eat while we were fishing. Granny would always fix us basket lunches, country ham and biscuit, boiled eggs and fried apple pies and a jar of pickles. The last thing she would say was "If you don't bring the basket back I won't fix you any more lunches." The basket was a big wicker basket with a handle. She used it to gather her eggs. She would go to the ice box, take the ice pick and chip off some ice to put in a gallon jug, wrap it with paper and it would stay cold all day. In those days we did not have electricity. It was 3 miles to the river. It was part of the old river. It was a big bend that had deep watter in the center it was 20 ft. deep. Dill and I would catch roaches, Granddad used them to catch bream. Dill and I would dig us a bucket of earthworms. We liked to fish for catfish.

Miss Lizzy and the Catfish

Luthur Smith lived by himself on the river bank. He made his living fishing and trapping. Old Luke, that is what most people called him. Luke would find hollow sypress logs. He would float them into shallow watter next to a deep hole. He would chop a hole in a log next to the bank. He called that his peep hole. He would leave the big end open next to the deep watter. The big catfish liked to nest in the log. They would go in to lay their eggs. One day I was fishing at the deep hole. I saw Old Luke floating a log into the bank. He didn't see me, if he had he would not have stopped there. I stayed real still until he was gone. Old Dan my bull dog was sitting next to me. I put my hand over his mouth so he could not bark.

About 2 weeks later, when I went fishing again, I decided to check old Luke's log. When I looked in I saw the largest catfish I had ever seen. I eased away, I didn't want to scare it. When I got home I went down to Dill's house. I told him that I had seen a catfish in Old Luke's log that would way 50 lbs. It had started raining so we couldn't work in the cotton next day. I told Dill to get a 9 ft. pick sack and we would stretch it over the open end of the log. He could hold the sack and I would take a stick and punch the fish and run it in to the sack.

We carried a plow line to tie onto the pick sack. We then tied the rope to a bush by the log. When I punched the cat-fish the log exploded. When it hit the end of the sack it jerked Dill into the watter. All I could see was Dill's feet, the fish was headed for deep watter. I ran back to the bush and got a hold

6

on the rope. I was able to pull the fish and Dill back to shallow watter. I asked Dill why he didn't turn the sack loose, he said he didn't have time, when the fish hit the end of the sack, it was just like a bull.

We both got hold of the rope and pulled the fish out on the bank. We opened the sack and looked in. It was one big catfish. I asked Dill what it would way. His eyes were big as saucers. He said "Good God, I think he will way 100 lbs." You could have put your head in its mouth. We didn't know how we were going to get the fish on the mule's back, I told Dill that I saw some blocks of wood over on the road. I guess they fell off some woodcutter's wagon. We got 4 blocks. I tied the rope to the horse's saddle. I told Dill to put 2 of the blocks under the fish when I pulled it off the ground. I put the other 2 blocks in the end of the sack to make a counter balance and tied the end. We both got on the horse and started for home. We were doing ok, when the fish flopped, the mule jumped and the fish slid back to the ground. We had to do the whole thing over after about 2 hours we made it 2 miles to the creek.

It was about 2 miles from home. We decided to give the fish a drink. We pulled the fish into the watter and were standing with the rope in our hand. We heard someone up on the bridge holler "What are you doing down there?" It was Old Man Bob Hodgy. We told him we had caught a big cat fish and there was another one still in the watter. He came sliding down the bank and looked in the sack. He let out a yell that sounded like an Indian. He said "Did you say that you saw another one like that in the hole?" We said "Yes we think it was larger, but don't tell anyone we are going to try to catch it tomorrow."

Old Man Bob always knew everything. Miss Lizzy was his wife. Old Man Bob and Miss Lizzy had a 30A (acre) farm on a back road. Bob didn't ever fix his fences. He had four cows and 2 horses. He raised about 5A of corn in a valley by the creek. He had the cornfield fenced to keep the cows and horses out. He didn't fix the pasture fences. If his cows got out and got into someone else's crops, the farmer wouldn't call Bob. They would just put Bob's cows in their pastures. They knew if they called Bob and he came and got them they would be back in their crops the next day. They decided it was better to pasture them free.

Old Man Bob climbed the bank and took off in a run. Miss Lizzy always wore a long black dress that came down to her shoes. Old Man Bob went strait home. He went to the barn and got four broken sacks. He unraveled them, sewed them together and made a sein. He got 2 willow sticks, put one on each end to pull the sein with, and got his log chain and wired it to the bottom to hold the sein down to the creek bottom. He hitched his mules to the wagon, put the sein in the wagon.

He went in the house to get Miss Lizzy. Miss Lizzy wasn't ready. He set in the porch swing and waited. Bob and Miss Lizzy had a bungolo house with a porch on all four sides. Miss Lizzy had a big rocking chair. She would move it to where a breeze was blowing. After 5 minutes he went back in the house. Miss Lizzy still was not ready. He could not stand it any longer. He hollered at Miss Lizzy to hurry up. "If we don't get that catfish this evening, Jack and Dill will get it early in the morning." Miss Lizzy put on her high top shoes on and got in the wagon.

When they got to the creek, Old Bob helped Lizzy slide down the creek bank. He went back to the wagon and got the sein. He slid down the creek bank and unrolled the sein. He gave one stick that the sein was tied to to Lizzy and said for her to walk along the bank. He waded across the creek. He told Lizzy to stay on the bank and she wouldn't get wet. Miss Lizzy was doing good, but when she got to the steep bank she began to slide, in the creek she went. Old Bob had to wade back to the other side. He caught Miss Lizzy's arm and pulled her back on the bank. Helped her to stand but the watter running out of her clothes made the ground slicker, the first step she took she slid back in the watter. Old Bob got her by the arm and pulled her out of the watter. Miss Lizzy was a devout member of the foot washing Baptist church. But by this time she had lost all of her religion. She called Old Bob names that no one had heard of.

The mail carrier was crossing the bridge about this time. He heard all of the noise under the bridge. He got out of his car and looked under the bridge. Ben Smith was the mailman. When he saw the shape Miss Lizzy was in he called to her to stand still. He got a long pole and slid down the bank. Miss Lizzy got one end of the pole and Ben Smith pulled Miss Lizzy back up the bank. Miss Lizzy was muddy from head to foot she had so much mud on her face she could hardly open her eyes. Old Bob crawled up the bank with the sein. Ben Smith asked Bob "What are you doing seining the creek?" Bob told him about the big catfish that Jack and Dill had caught in the creek. Ben Smith said "Hell Bob, those boys were pulling your leg. They didn't catch that fish in the creek." Bob helped Miss Lizzy into the wagon. The last thing Ben heard, Miss Lizzy was giving Old Bob hell. By the time Ben Smith finished his mail route, everyone had heard about Old Bob and the big catfish.

The next day after Miss Lizzy helped Bob sein for the big cat fish Bob made his regular appearance at the store. Everyone wanted to know if he caught the big catfish. He said "Hell no, but he is in there and I saw his mate." He said "Jack and Dill had a plow line tied through his mouth and was leading him around. I asked them where they caught it and they said in the creek. They said they saw his mate. I sure as hell would have caught it if Lizzy hadn't fell in the creek." Everyone was laughing at Bob, but there was no way to convince him that Jack and Dill had not caught the big fish in the creek.

After Old Bob left to get Miss Lizzy I told Dill to get on the horse and go home. I said for him to get my uncle Leo to bring the T-Ford. I would stay with the fish. In about 1 hour Leo and Dill arrived in the T-Ford. We loaded the catfish in the back of the Ford. Dill got on the mule and we all left for home. When we got home we got the cotton scales, we got some bailing wire, tied the scales to the rafters in the car shed. Josh [Dill's daddy] and Leo tied the cotton sack to the cotton scale to way the fish. It wayed 56 lbs. After the fish was cleaned we had 2 dish pans full of cat fish stakes.

The next day it had rained and they could not work in the fields so we all had a fish fry. The men got the wash pot out and started a fire under it. They went to the smoke house and got a stand [a five gallon bucket] of lard. Dill's sister Cindy and the women were in the house helping Granny, some were pealing potatoes and onions. Some were helping Granny with the fresh fried apple pies. When the pot was boiling the potatoes were rolled in salt & black pepper and corn meal and dropped in the pot of boiling grease. When the potatoes came to the top golden brown they were ready to eat. The catfish was rolled in corn meal with salt and black pepper added. It was put in the hot grease.

When it was all ready, Granny asked Granddad to say the blessing. Granddad was hard of hearing. He thought she said was he ready to eat, he said hell yes he was ready to eat. He had been starving for an hour. Dill's mom Mary got up and said the blessing. She was more than thankful for Dill and Jack catching the big fish. Granny and the women had fried 2 dozen fresh apple pies. Dill's moma, Mary, had brought a big pot of fresh black eyed peas. We also had a big pot of fresh boiled corn. There was a big dish of sliced red ripe tomatoes.

The men went to the shop and got saw horses. They placed them under the shade trees. They went to the lumber stock and got plankes to lay over the saw horses to make tables. Everyone went to the wood pile and got a round block of wood to sit on. Everyone enjoyed the good food.

In those days everyone had it rough. No one had any money, they worked hard, raised their own food. No one had any bills to pay at that time and no one had electricity. One gallon of kerosine or coal oil would last a month. It cost a dime.

The hardest thing for most land owners to pay were land taxes. Cotton would bring 5¢ per lb—$25 a bale. If you got behind on your land tax the county court would sell your farm for taxes. Every month the paper would have a list of farms to be auctioned off at the front door of the court house. My Granddad bought a farm from Mr. John Parker. I remember a statement that Mr. Parker made. He said "Frank I am going to be the poorest man in the county. I own more land than any one else. I do not get enough rent to pay the taxes. I am getting farther in debt each year."

When the Depression hit my Granddad had 10 Registered Jersey cows. He gave over $100 for each one. All you could get for a 1 year old Heifer was $5. Granddad said he would not sell one for that. In 2 years we had 20 cows to milk, morning and p.m. Each family had to send some one to each milking. They would each bring a bucket to take their milk home in. The rest of the milk we gave to Granny. What she didn't want we gave to the hogs. The next year they built a cheese factor in Dyersburg. The truck would pick up the milk and take it to the cheese factory.

Granny Taught us our Lessons

Granddad lived $1\frac{1}{2}$ miles on a dirt road. When you got to main road it was another $1\frac{1}{2}$ mi. to the school house. It was 2 more miles to Dill's school at Rock Springs. Rock Springs was a settlement where several negroes had small farms. In the winter time when the roads were muddy, we stayed home. Granny had a blackboard and some crayons. Dill and Cindy would come up to the house. We would use my books. Granny would give us a list of 25 spelling words. She would give us 30 mins. to study them. She would take the list away and have us write them on paper. We were penalized for the words we missed. Cindy was a good speller and I would try to get a look at her paper. She would keep it covered so we couldn't see it.

Granny would put sweet potatoes in a pan by the fire place. When the juice started running out they were ready to eat. We always gathered pecans, walnuts and hickory nuts in the fall. We would vote on which kind we were going to have each day. We would crack the nuts and pick the meats out. Granny would get sorgum molasses, put the nut in with molasses and make hard candy. On other days we would pop popcorn and Granny would make popcorn balls with sorgum molasses.

After we ate our lunch we would have a domino game. Granny would have each one of us take turns keeping score. Dill and I would play Granny and Cindy. On the days when Cindy had to help her mother, Leo or Granddad would play dominoes with us.

"Watch That Goat!"

My Granddad always would keep some goats in the barn. He thought the goat smell would keep the fleas away. One day on a fishing trip I found some coaster wagon wheels on the community dump. I brought them home and Dill and I made a wagon. We fixed some harness for Granddad's goat, Old Bill. We could not figure out how to catch Old Bill. When you got him cornered he would turn and butt you down. I had to call Old Dan, my bull dog. All I had to say was "Ketch the goat." He would get Old Bill by one of his ears and lead him around. While Dan held Old Bill we would put the harness on him and hitch him to the wagon. I would tell Dan to let the goat go. When Dan turned the goat loose he would not move. Old Bill had some balls hanging down about 6 inches. I told Dill to get a weed and tickle his balls. That did the trick. He just couldn't stand to have his balls tickled. He would take off in a run.

The shed that we used for a car shed had a long pole on one side for a brace. Old Bill could walk the pole and get on top of the car shed. He got so every time we went into the horse lot, Old Bill would head for the car shed. If he caught you not looking he would slip up behind you and butt you.

One day Dill and I were playing leap frog. One would reach down and catch his ankles, the other would place his hand on his back. Then the other would do the same thing. I had just jumped over Dill when I looked up, Old Bill was coming at us full speed. He lowered his head and hit Dill square in the ass. He knocked Dill 2 flips. All you had to say to Dill to make him jump was "Watch that goat!"

One morning I was carrying a bucket of milk and Old Bill caught me in the rear. The milk bucket went one way, and I went the other. From then on when I went into the horse lot, I had the bull dog with me. The other goats didn't pay us any mind. One day Granddad said if you don't keep that bull dog out of the horse lot, I am not going to have any young goats. You keep Old Bill on the card shed all the time.

Building a Boiler

When we were planting it was my or Dill's job to ride the drag. The drag was made with 6 wide planks nailed on a 2 x 4 runner. It was fixed so you could hitch a mule to it. Then you would put some sacks of dirt on the drag for weight. I would get on the drag and drag down 2 rows at a time. The planter would follow and plant the smooth rows. In those days everyone would save their cotton seed at the gin.

Granddad had a side shed he put the cotton seed in. He would feed some to the milk cows, but always made sure he saved enough to plant 2 times. The gin was an old steam gin. It had a steam whistle. Old Man Lum Street fired the boilers. He would blow the steam whistle at 12 o'clock sharp. Everyone would set their clock by Lum's whistle.

One day after the gin season was over, James Powell and I were down at the gin. We found a steam clock that had been discarded. We found a 2 gallon bucket. We sautered the clock to the bucket. We filled the bucket ½ full with watter. We sautered the lid on the bucket. We found some brick, we went down to the creek bank and fixed a furnace. We wanted to see how much steam the bucket would hold.

We built a fire under the bucket and I was watching the steam clock. Just about the time I said 8 lbs the bucket blew up. The steam clock hit me in the head. I had overalls on. I pulled them off and jumped in the creek. I had a straw hat on and I was looking down, that saved my face. James had his back to the furnace and he got a scalded ass. I stayed in the creek until I got cool. I didn't have many blisters. After I had cooled off I went home buck naked. I went down the road with my overalls in one hand and my straw hat in the other. Back then everyone thought cold watter was the worst thing you could do for a burn. But now they say it's the right thing to do.

Learning to Swim

One day some older boys were going to the river to go swimming. I wanted to go with them but they said I couldn't go because I could not swim. I told them I had learned how. When we got to the river I was standing on the bridge, watching the others swim. One of the older boys slipped up behind me. He pitched me over the banister. It was a 20 ft drop to the watter. When I came up I started fighting the watter. From then on I was not scared of the watter and I could swim. At that time there was no swimming pools. If you went swimming you went to the river or someone's pond.

Aunt Molly

Aunt Molly was a visitor. She visited everyone black and white. You could always see her with her walking cane in all kinds of weather. It would take her all day to get through the village. She would stop at everyone's houses. If there were sick folks she would send for her clothes.

Aunt Molly had a sister everyone called her Dinky. They had a 20 acre farm 2 miles from RoEllen a village of about 100 people. She had two cows, a sow, pigs and about 100 chickens. In the spring time all the men would have an Aunt Molly Day. They would take their lunches and plant her farm. She would have 2 acres of cotton, 3 acres of corn, 1/2 acre of stock peas. She would pick peas when they got dry on the stalk. Then she would pull the vines and stack them for hay in the winter. She would have 6 acres for pasture, and 4 acres for hay. When the jap had seeded up they would gather, blacks and whites, cut and stack the hay, gather the corn, put it in her small barn. There was no collar borrow [color barrier], everybody worked together. You could leave your doors open. There were few thieves. If one was caught he had to leave the community no one would give him work.

One day we got a deep snow. Luke Jones came over to my house. He was in my grade in school. He had a half grey-hound and half bird dog. We went over to Granddad and picked up Old Dan. Dill had a small dog that would get in the bryer patches and ditches. We used the dogs to catch the rabbits. In those day there were rabbits everywhere. That was before they used any poison raising a crop. We each had a long stick. If the rabbit got close enough to us, we would kill it with our sticks.

It was about 3 miles to Aunt Molly's farm. We got to her house just about 11 o'clock. We each had our own rabbits. I had 5, Luke had 5 and Dill had 7. After carrying those rabbits in the deep snow, we were really tired. When we got to Aunt Molly's house I knocked on the door. I asked her if she wanted some rabbits. She said '"Boy you know I want some rabbits.'" We went out to the side shed and dressed the rabbits. When we got back in the house, Dill was still holding his rabbits. I asked him if he was going to give Aunt Molly his rabbits. He said no he was not hungry.

Aunt Molly had a pot of white beans on her woodstove. She made 2 pans of homemade biscuits and a big bowl of brown gravy. While Aunt Molly was doing the cooking, Luke and I went to the wood pile. We got her cross cut saw and sawed a big pile of wood. While we were cutting the wood, Dill was carrying it into the house and stacking it behind the stove. When we got the wood cut, we went back in the house. Aunt Molly had a big pan full of fried rabbit it was golden brown. When you opened the door it almost took your breath away. It smelled so good. We all pulled a chair up to the kitchen table and started eating. We would cover those hot brown biscuits with gravy. We had white beans and a big red onion.

I looked back at Dill. He had said he was not hungry. He was going to the sell his rabbits for 10 cents a piece. After the second round, Dill saw how the gravy and biscuits were leaving. He just couldn't stand it any more. He said Aunt Molly I done changed my mind. I am going to give you my rabbits too. I knew he could not stand not to eat. There are two things that black people like best, catfish and rabbit.

We hunted all the way back to Granddad's house. We had 5 rabbits a piece when we got back. We cleaned them and carried them to the store. We each had 50 cents. The store building was a huge 2 story wood building. In the middle was an iron pole that went to the top of the building. Mr. Ed Davis owned the business. He had several farms. He had a hole in his throat. He had to put his finger over the hole before he could talk. He would get me to go with him from farm to farm. I would open the gates for him. He had an A model Ford Coupe. He would tell me to get me something to eat and a cold drink. I would get me a Baby Ruth and a big coke.

Tom Cribbs and Clay Joshlin were the clerks. They would get hog lard and a ladder and grease the iron pole. They would give you a free coke if you could climb the pole. I saw a pile of sand out back where they had bored a new well. I filled my overall's pockets with sand and went into the store. Old Clay Joshlin said Jack do you want to climb the pole for a coke. I said I would climb it for 2 cokes. I had decided that I was not going to fool them but once so I had better get two cokes of out of it. I had some tennis shoes on. I got some sand on the shoes. When I got started up the pole a crowd gathered

16

around. No one had climbed the pole before. I went up the pole like a squirrel each time I would start to slip I would reach in my pocket and get some more sand. When I reached the top there was a big roar.

Mr. Ed called me back in his office. He said "Jack tell me how you tricked them." I reached in my pocket and pulled out some sand. He laughed and laughed. He said "I knew if anyone could beat them you could." When I got home my mother was so mad, I had grease all over my overalls. She said you just put them on clean this morning. She said pull them off and put on some more.

Old Mack and the Birddog

The point behind this joke is that the dog was supposed to point birds only.

I had a single shot 22 rifle. Rube Featherston had a good bird dog named Mack. Almost everyone owned a bird dog then. No one put dogs in a pen. They just ran free. I would get behind Rube's barn and call Old Mack. I would take him a rabbit hunting. He would find and point the rabbits, and I would shoot them with the 22 rifle while they were sitting. Rube had a small ice cream parlor and grocery store. He had a huge wood stove in the center of the floor. At night all of the bird hunters would gather around the stove and tell their hunting tales. After I had taken Old Mack rabbit hunting I would go to Rube's store and listen to the hunting tales, Rube would say "I just can't understand Old Mack, all he wanted to do today was point rabbits." Finis Elgen always went hunting with Rube. Finis would say "Hell Rube he didn't just want to point the rabbits he wanted to run them." Rube would call Old Mack in and give him a whipping. When the day was just about over Mack would start pointing quail.

Dr. Hall

We had one doctor in a 5 mi. radius. His name was Dr. Hall. He would make house calls day and night. He had an A model Roadster. He took the lid off the turtle hull [rumble seat] and put a wire cage in its place. Nobody had any cash so they would give him chickens, eggs, country ham. If they gave him a calf or pig they had to deliver it to his house. He doctored blacks and whites alike. It is funny how good blacks and whites got along. No one had any cash, but they were all willing to help each other. If anyone was in need there was always some one to give him help.

In the winter time the dirt roads were so muddy, Dr. Hall would have to ride a horse. Drs. in those days didn't have anything but home remedies. In the winter time there was a lot of newmonia. It was an infection in the lungs. There was a four day critical time. If you made it past the fourth day, you usually died or started getting better. If you had a broken leg or arm, you had to go to Dr. Hall's house. The thing that people dreaded most was a flu epidemic. People don't realize that before the discovery of sulpher drugs and penicillin in the 1940s there was no cure for any infection.

Dr. Hall's favorite saying was "I always watch the top crop of the cotton. It is the last that is picked and I am the last to get paid. If the top crop is short, I have a rough winter." He knew he was going to have a tough winter anyway, with muddy roads and getting stuck. He said he was glad the farmers were not busy in the winter. That way all of the babies would come in the summer and fall. If there were any born in the winter, the neighbor women or Aunt Molly would have to deliver them.

It would be impossible to make the young people understand just how hard times were in the early 1930's, but I think everyone enjoyed life even if it was a rough one. Back then if you worked you ate. If anyone needed help, the whole community pitched in, black or white. But if you were lazy and wouldn't work, it was a different story.

18

Food

Everyone had plenty of milk and butter, dried peas and beans, canned tomatoes. Most everyone had a root seller, where they stored Irish potatoes, sweet potatoes and turnips. We usually had a huge turnip patch. Granny would pick a big bucket of greens. She would wash them good at the pump. She would put a big slice of country ham in her cast iron pot, put about 1/4 full of watter in it, to that she would add 4 pods of cian pette [cayenne pepper]. She would put the greens on the stove and let them boil slow for about 3 hrs. She would then take the extra juice and put that in another pot she would add 1/4 cup of sugar and some black pepper. She would peel her turnips, dice them and cook them in the juice. She always had a platter of country ham and a platter of country sausage in the warming closet at the top of the stove. When you had a skillet of corn bread to go with that you had some fine eating.

Granddad always had an orchard. Granny would can the peaches and plums and strawberries and black berries. The apples would be sliced then Granny would get a white sheet, it was my job to spread the sheet on the tin roof of the shed. I would take the apples up to the shed and spread them out on the sheet. They would stay on the shed until just before sun down. Then I would have to bring them down for the night. The same procedure I would go through for 4 to 5 days. Granny would use them to make fried apple pies in the winter.

Granddad always would have bee hives at one end of the orchard. I was always careful not to upset them. Old Dan would always be hunting rabbits, close to the hives and upset them. The bees would get mad and hunt someone to sting. One day Old Dan ran into a hive and turned it over. Dan started running toward me. He had bees all over his head and back. When he got close enough for me to see him, he decided the best thing for him to do was roll in the grass. When he did the bees all started after me. I ran as hard as I could but I still got four or five stings. Granddad found the

19

bee hive turned over and he was mad as hell. He said he was going to shoot that damn bull dog if I didn't keep him out of the orchard.

Reelfoot Lake

Reelfoot Lake is in the northwest corner of Tennessee. It was formed during the Earthquakes of 1811 and 1812. It is the center of the New Madrid fault. It was thought to be the largest quake we ever had in the U.S.A. The land was covered with huge sypress trees, some were 100 ft. tall. The lake ran from the Mississippi River on the west to the high cliffs on the east. It was 40 mi. long and 20 mi. wide. It was in 1928 and I was 11 years old. My Granddad had always heard about the good fishing in Reelfoot Lake, he decided he and I should take a week and find out if it was true. He had just bought a new T-model Ford. Granddad had a friend that had spent a week on the lake. He contacted him and found out where he stayed at the lake. There were no hotels or motels at the lake back then. The place was more like a modern bed and breakfast. He wrote the family and made a reservation for a week.

We put out roach traps. We had a lard stand with holes punched in it so the roaches could get air. We put stale bread and Irish potatoes for them to eat on, we also put a large spunge in the bottom so they could get watter. We put some damp straw over the spung. Each day Dill and I would run the roach traps and put them in the lard stand. We also had a large pile of leafs we would add some dry manure to the leafs. About 2 days each week we would pore some watter over the pile. This way we had fishing worms in the summertime every day. Dill would say "I sho do wish I could go to Reelfoot Lake with you." I would tell him to just keep the worm pile wattered and we would go fishing at the old river when I got back.

Granddad's friend said we had better take our own bate. There were no bate shops over there at that time. We were supposed to go on Sunday, Granny fixed us a big lunch basket. We loaded our fishing gear and bate into the T-Ford. We took a change of clothes in a bag. It was about 40 mi. to the lake. We left early and got there about 12 noon. The roads were pretty rough in places. We ate a picnick lunch on the lake shore. After that we found the house where we were to spend the week.

It was about ¼ of a mile from the spillway. The spillway was a huge cannall that let the excess water out of the lake. The lake was deep then, about 1/4 of the huge sypress trees were still out of the watter. It was a natural fish hatchery. There were almost all kinds of wild life around the lake. There was an island that had eagles nests on it. I did all my fishing at the spillway, where the watter runs out of the lake. I fished at the base of the watter fall. You would catch all kinds of fish there.

The people where we stayed were farmers. We would take our fish in at night and dress or clean them. We had fish every night. That was the first time I ever ate any turtle. I caught a lotts of catfish at the spillway, most were channel cat. They are a good eating fish.

There has been a big change at Reelfoot Lake since then, that was 70 years ago. You have motells and restaurants everywhere. They also have an airport. The lake is about 1/4 the depth it was back then. The silt from the cultivated fields has almost filled the lake in some places.

We had a good week of fishing, but I was glad to see the T-Ford the next Sunday. We made it home before dark. Granny and Old Dan were sure glad to see us. I was glad to get back to Granny's cooking. I had all of the catfish and turtle I needed for a spell.

Dill wanted me to tell him about my fishing trip to Reelfoot Lake. I said just about any place you put your hook you would catch a fish. Dill said that he and Cindy were caught up chopping cotton. He said he would sure like to go fishing at the old river. We caught the old horse. We would have to ride him, the share croppers were using all of the mules. We found an empty can in the trash barrell and filled it half full with worms. We filled the rest of the way with moist leafs. We got our fishing poles, Granny brought us a gallon bucket filled with country ham and biscuits and cookies. We got a small jug and I filled it with watter. We put all of our food and watter up on the edge of the tool shed.

We both got on the horse and rode the horse up to the shed. We had a snap on each side of the saddle. We strapped the food and watter to each side of the saddle. We were ready to go. Old Dan always followed along behind.

We were doing fine untill we got to Tom Bunn's house. The house was about ½ mile off the road. He had 2 big black hounds. He was a coon hunter. The hounds would run down to the road barking, when anyone came down the road. I called Dan up close to the horse, for I didn't have time for a dog fight. It looked like I had everything under controll, but one of the hounds got too close to the horse. I could not controll Dan any moore. The hound was no match for the bull dog. I had to get off the horse. I knew old Dan would kill the hound if I didn't get him off. Dan had the hound on his back on the ground. He had a death grip on the hound's throat. I kicked Dan with my foot but that didn't do any good. I saw that the hound was not going to last very long if I didn't get Dan loose from his throat.

I decided to grab Dan by the balls and twist them. When I did that he loosened his grip on the hound's throat. The hound was able to get loose from Dan. He made a beeline for his house. Tom Bunn came running down to the road. He had his shot gun with him. He said he was going to shoot that dam bull dog. I said "If you shoot my dog you are going to have to shoot me." He decided he had better think things over. He knew if he shot my dog, that Granddad would come after him with his shot gun. He said "You boys go on fishing, I guess it was my dog's fault after all."

We went on down to the river. After we got to the river we put the horse on a long leed line and tied him to a tree. We had some fishing lines already fixed. We cut us some long canes, striped off the leaves, tied on the lines, baited hooks with worms and pitched the bait as far as you could in the watter and stuck the canes in the river bank. We each had four poles to watch.

We brought a tow or crocker sack to put the fish in. We would make a slip noose around the open end of the sack. When we would catch a fish we would pull the sack to the bank. We had a long string tied to the sack and to a sharp stick we pushed into the river bank. We had been fishing for 2 hrs. We had caught several fish. We decided it was time to eat our lunch. We had country ham, biscuits, and cookies. We also had our pockets full of apples. We caught several more fish while we were eating.

The last time we pulled the sack a huge snake was wrapped around it When he saw us, he fell back into the watter. Old Dan saw the snake. He sat on the bank watching, the snake could smell the fish in the sack. The next time we pulled the sack out of the watter the snake came up the bank after it. That was a mistake he shouldn't have made. Old Dan grabbed the snake behind the head and shook him to several pieces.

We had a sack about ½ full so we decided it was time to go home. When we got to Tom Bunn's place we didn't see anything of the hounds. I am sure those hounds had all of that bull dog they could stand. When we got home I gave Dill all of the Polly catfish. I am sure they had catfish for 2 days. I cleaned 10 bream and 10 croppie. Granddad liked the bream. I liked the croppie. Granny rolled them in corn meal with salt added and fried them in a big cast iron skillet.

The next day I went by the tomato patch where Dill and Cindy were picking tomatoes. Dill and I had been talking about the big snake that Old Dan had caught. By the time we got through with the tale we had the snake 8 ft. long and as big around as a gallon bucket. Cindy usually acted like she was not paying any attention to what we were saying. But we knew that she was, especially if you were talking about snakes. Cindy was all bent over picking tomatoes. I found a long weed. I eased it up under Cindy's dress and hollered snake. She ran all over the basket of tomatoes. She was hollering like a wild, wild Indian. I caught up with her. She said she was going up to Granny's and tell her what I did. I had a Baby Ruth candy bar that I had been saving for 2 days. I told Cindy if she wouldn't tell Granny I would give her the candy.

Old Dan and the Bull

Granny needed Dill and I to go to the country store for her. She got her tablet and pincell and wrote down the things she needed. She gave me the list and the money and I put it in my overalls pocket. We were going to walk. I told Dill we were going to put geomitry to the walk. He said "What the hell is geomitry? Is it good to eat?" I got a stick and drew our road out by John McGrow's house. "There we hit the main road from RoEllen to Dyersburg. At John McGrow's house we turn right." I told him Geneva my older sister has showed me a straight line is the shortest distance between 2 points. "We go straight across John McGrow's cow pasture and we will cut our walk in half." Dill said "I ain't going into that pasture, you nose old man John has got a mean Jersey bull in that pasture." I said I was not scared for this time of day the bull would be in the barn in the shade.

We walked up to the pasture fence. We did not see any sign of the bull. We crawled under the fence and were about half way across the pasture when we heard the bull snort. He was pawing the ground and throwing dirt over his back. We started running to a small persimon tree. We had just climbed about 8 ft from the ground when the bull hit the tree. I looked over at Dill and his eyes were big as coffee cups. The bull snorted and backed off for another try. When he hit the tree persimons fell all over the ground but we were still up in the tree. The bull backed off and snorted pawing the ground.

Dill said "You done got us in a hell of a mess. What is we going to do?'" I saw old Dan back at the fence, digging after a mole. I hollered "Dan" as loud as I could. He looked up and saw the bull pawing the dirt. He made a beeline for the bull and caught him by the nose. The bull bellowed and began shaking his head, but Old Dan held on. The bull's nose was bleeding bad. I hollered for Dan to turn the bull loose. When Dan turned the bull loose he bellowed and started running to the barn. We climbed down and started on across the pasture. Dill said "My legs are so weak I don't know if I can walk."

We walked on to the store. We got the things Granny wanted and we had a dime left over. I gave Dill a nickel and I had a nickel. I bought me some jaw breakers, I wanted something to last. Dill said "Ise going to get me a Baby Ruth. I been wanting one since Cindy got yours over the snake deal." When we got ready to go home Dill said "I am going to stay on the road. I don't give a dam abut the geomitry road." By the time we got back to John McGrows house Dill had eaten all his Baby Ruth bar. I still had four of my jaw breakers left. Dill said I sure would like one of your jaw breakers. We turned on our road home. We had to go by the lot where the bull was. He was laying in the hall of the barn his nose was still bleeding. He did not get up. He had all of the bull dog that he wanted.

That night John McGrow called Grannie's. We had an old crank tellephone. Granddad was hard of hearing and could not talk on the phone. He told Granny what Dan had done to his bull's nose. He said to tell Jack not to bring that bull dog in his pasture any more. It was about 10 days later that Miss Nancy, John McGrow's wife, called Granny on the phone. She was crying so Granny could hardly hear her. She said tell Jack to bring the bull dog. The Jersey bull had John down in the hall of the barn and she was afraid to go in the lot. I got on the old horse and called Dan. When we got there John McGrow had gotten under the feed trough that ran along the side of the barn. The bull was snorting and pawing but he couldn't reach him. I got up on the lot gate and told Dan to get the bull. He started across the lot, but the bull saw him. The bull put his tail over his back and started running to the back of the pasture.

By that time the news had gotten around and several people had gotten there. On the party line every one listened in, so the news got around. Four men got John out from under the feed trough and carried him into the house. He was bruised up pretty good, but no bones were broken. He called me into the house and thanked me for coming to his rescue and Miss Nancy gave me a big piece of chocolate cake. I sat down and ate my cake and drank a glass of milk. That Sunday the Baptist preacher's sermon was about the Good Lord and a good bull dog named Dan.

Fish Fry

In the summer time on the 4th of July, every one would go down to the Forked Deer River for a fish fry. Aunt Molly looked forward to the fish fry. Some one would always go after Aunt Molly and Lizzy. There would be wagons, cars, and horses every where. The wemon would fry country ham and make jugs of ice tea. They would bring iron kettles to cook the fish and the french fries in. There would be a pot to boil the sweet corn in. Each wagon would bring too or three planks in the bottom of the wagon bed. The men would cut poles and set them in the ground to make tables for the food and a place to eat. The men would bring a roll of hog wire. There was a large sand bar in the river. They would take the wire to the side of the sand bar where there was not any current. There was always some one watching to see that the small ones did not get out of the fenced in era. Kids, they could play in the sand and watter, but if they got in the current, they would be swept down the river.

Ruffus, Effus, and Grant were Aunt Mollys cousins. They always brought Aunt Molly and Lizzy. Ruffus, Effus and Grant would not get in the river and help catch the fish. They would bring the wash tubs to the river bank, the men in the river would empty the sacks of fish into the tubs. You would need too men with sacks in the watter. Each time they would catch a fish, they would put it into the feed sack. Ruffis, Effus and Grant were not going to get into the water they were ascared of the snakes.

The men would use tramble nets to catch the fish. They would circle the drifts in the river with the tramble nets, then they would get inside of the circle with punch poles and run the fish into the nets. The fish were mostly carp and buffalo, they would way five to ten pounds most of the time. They would catch a few yellow catfish. Some of them would weigh twenty lbs.

The wemon all brought chairs. There were trees along the river banks, and they would set in the shade. The people would all get together or on the telephone and decide what each one should bring. They would need too stands of lard to cook the fish and the french fries in. Ruffus, Effus and Grant would clean a wash tub of fish, they would get the fires going under the wash kettles. They would have dish pans with corn-meal, salt and pepper. They would drop the pieces of fish into the corn meal and roll them around to get them covered with meal. They would drop the pieces of fish into the boiling greese. In about ten minutes the pieces of fish would rise to top, golden brown and ready to take out of the greese and eat.

When the first tub of fish were ready to eat the wemon and kidds would eat. They had all kinds of pickles and pre-serves. There is no fish as good tasting as those fresh out of the watter and into the frying pan. It was hard to get the men out of the watter, they enjoyed catching the fish as much as they did eating them. After the third tub full was caught they would quit, and bring the tramble net out on the bank. Effus, Ruffus and Grant had already eaten, and they would keep cooking fish as long as any one would eat them. Grandady would say "Effus, how do the fish tast?" Effus would say "If they tasted any better I couldn't stand it."

This was a day of hard work, good eating and a lotts of fun. Every body black and white enjoyed the day. Every one pitched in and cleaned up the camp ground. They burried all of the scraps, and fish bones. They cleaned up the cooking kettles and buried the greese. By the middle of the evening every one was ready to start for home. It had been a very enjoyable day for every one. What amazes me now is that

27

every one has every thing but love and happyness. In those days the people did not have much money, but they did not have a drug culture and very little crime. There was no welfare, but no one went hungry. Every one worked hard and lived off the land. If any one got sick and needed help, the whole neighborhood would get together and help the family out. Those were the kind of people that settled the county, fought the wars and made the country great. During the great depression times were hard, no one had any money, but every one was in the same boat and you did the best you could and most people were happy. It's not that way with the next generation. They have everything and are bored with life.

J.T. Reagen and the Brick

Everyone had to walk to school, some as much as four or five miles. I was walking home one afternoon, with a boy named J.T. Reagen. He lived about 1 1/2 miles past my Granddad's place. He was about twice the size of everyone else in his class. He had a habbit of pushing everyone else around. He had caused me to drop my books, a couple of times that afternoon.

There was a high levy on the road as you cross the creek. The levy sides were grown up with weeds and black berry bryers. J.T. gave me a big shove off the road down in the bryers. I had bryers sticking in my face, hands and neck. As I was crawling up the levy bank, I saw a half of brick. I was crying and mad as hell. I got the brick and when I got on the road again J.T. was bent over laughing. I took the brick and hit him in the back of the head. He grabbed his head and when he saw all of the blood he started running. When he got to Granddad's house Granny tried to stop him to find out what was wrong with him. All he would say was "Jack hit me with a brick" and started running again. He thought I was still after him with the brick.

When I got to Grannies she was all shook up. She wanted to know why I had hit J.T. Reagen with a brick. I showed her my hands and face, with all the bryers still sticking in. I was bleeding just about as much as J.T. Granny sat me in a chair and picked the rest of the bryers out. My face looked like I had a fresh case of meazells by the time Granny got all of the bryers picked out of me.

The phone wrang. It was old lady Reagen calling Granny about Jack hitting J.T. in the head with a brick. Granny told her she was sorry, but if someone had pushed her in a bryer patch, she would have hit them with a brick too. Miss Reagen called Dr. Hall and he came and sewed J.T.'s head up. When Miss Reagen called Granny on the party line everyone in the community knew about it.

J.T. didn't get to go to school for two weeks. When he got back in school he was a different person. He didn't push anyone around anymore. J.T. came to me and said he was sorry he pushed me into the bryers. He said "Please don't hit me in the head with a brick again. You almost kilt me."

15 years later I was drafted into the army. I was at the induction station at Ft. Oglethorp GA. We were in the line for the physical exam and J.T. Reagen was just in front of me. He was classed 4F, I asked him if the brick got him exempted, he said he didn't know, but it could have.

The Hideway

One day Luke Jones, Dill and I were fishing on the creek. There was a high ridge that ran down to the creek. We decided to built us a cabin on the ridge next to the creek. We had to go by the cotton gin, that was located on the creek. Lumm Street was in charge of the crew repairing the gin. They had a large canvass tarp that come with some new machinery. I ask Lumm if we could have the tarp. He said "Take it on, if I dont give it to you, some one else will get it."

We went to Grandadys and got [the] old mule Jake. We put the harness on him and tied a feed sak on one side. We filled it with tools and used bailing wire. We carried a hatchet, some nails and a post hole digger. We needed a one man cross cut saw. We had so much tied on the mule we could not ride. We had to walk and lead him. The old mule sure did look funny, with all that stuff tied to him. When we got to the gin, we got some used 2x4 lumber and built a sled. We sawed one end of the 2x4s to make some runners. When we got the sled finished, we folded the tarp and placed it on the sled.

We found a piece of boiler plate in the scrap pile. I found Lumm Street and ask if we could have it. He said "You can have it but what in hell do you want with it." I said "We were going to build us a cooking stove with it." That piece of steel was heavy. We all three flipped it end over end, and finally got it on the sled. We got some used fire bricks out of the scrap pile and put them on the sled. We hitched Old Jake to the sled. We had so much piled on the sled that we would have to let old Jake rest about every five hundred yards. We had to cut a road part of the way, next to the creek. Someone had discarded some old car seats. After we unloaded the sled, we went back and got the car seats. We dug post holes about two feet deep.

We measured off a stick eight feet long. We cut willow trees 6 inches at the butt. We cut all of the limbs off each tree. We placed the butt end of the tree in each hole. We tamped the soil around each tree. We have five trees on each side, put the tarps over the trees and bent them together just like a covered wagon. We placed the ends side by side and wrapped them with used bailing wire. We cut two poles for each side. We wired them to each of the cross pieces to make the shell more stable. We placed one down the middle to act as a ridgerow. We unfolded the tarp and spread it over the frame. We put one pole on each side so we could roll the sides up if we needed more air. We placed the car seats along each side. We had our cabin finished. It looked just like a covered wagon. We called it the Hideaway.

We cut some sticks the same size as the piece of steel. We measured the ground and dug a hole about eighteen inches deep. We placed the fire brick along each side and the back. The fire brick were about four inches above the ground. We placed the boiler plate over the bricks and we had our cook stove made.

We took the sled apart. We made a table out of the 2x4s. We cut two of 2X4s in the center. We nailed one of the 2x4s the height we wanted for the table. Their were two trees eight feet apart. We then nailed 2 2x4's the height we wanted the seat, then we nailed two upright 2x4s to the pieces coming from the trees. That way we had supports for our table and seat. We had 8 2x4s for the table top and 4 for the seat. The seat seemed a little weak, so we cut a block of wood and placed it under the middle of the seat, that made the seat strong enough to hold up a Jersey bull. Dill said I sure will be glad when we get something to eat on our new table.

Granny had just put a new lanolium rug on her kitchen floor. She had to cut a piece ten feet long and three feet wide off one end to make the lannolium fit the kitchen floor. I asked Granny if we could have the piece that was left over. She said we could have it. We rolled it up and Dill and I caught the old horse, I got some roofing tacks and a hammer. We road down to the Hidaway and nailed the lanolium on the table top. Dill said "Boy we got us an uptown tabble. All we have to do is wash it off when the birds shit on it."

I told Dill that Luke Jones and I were going to put us a trotline in the creek late that afternoon. We had found a cotolfa tree covered with worms. Catfish like cotolfa worms better than anything. Dill said he could not help, he had to help his dady cut fire wood for the winter. Late that afternoon Luke and I went down to the creek. We carried a large tin can and filled it with cotalfa worms. We cut too large canes. We tied ten fish hooks about three feet apart on a line we had tied to the canes. We put a worm on each hook. I tied a used rail road spike in the center of the line to hold the line close to the bottom. Catfish like to feed next to the bottom. I took one cane and Luke took the other. We had sharpened each of the canes so we could stick them in the creek bank, this placed the trotline in the center of the creek.

We decided to have a fish dinner at the Hidaway the next day. I said "Luke we dont have anything to cook the fish in." He said his mother had an old cast iron skillett that she did not use any more. "I think I can talk her into giving it to me." Granny gave me some corn meal in a paper sack she put some salt and pepper in the meal. I went to the smoke house and cut four slices of country ham just in case we didn't catch any fish. I put some Irish potatoes and onions in a sack and I was ready to go.

When I got to Lukes house, I realized I did not have any greese to cook the fish in. Luke got an empty coffee can and filled it with lard and we were on our way. We were anxious to see how manny fish we had caught. When we got to the creek and were almost to the Hideaway, we heard somone laughing and splashing in the creek. We sliped up to the creek behind some trees. When we looked over the bank there were too girls in the creek buck nacked. I made like I had not seen them. I said "Luke I wonder whose these clothes belong to." I stood up and they got on their knees with the watter up to their chens. We sat down on the bank like we were going to spend the day. The oldest one of the girls, really got mad. She said "I dont give a damn if you do see me necked. I am coming out of this creek. I am going down to the blacksmith shop and tell my Uncle Ben, he lives up over the blacksmith shop and we are visiting him."

The girls lived in the Mississippi bottoms. That was before the big levy was built and the watter got high every spring. We told the girls that we were going to leave and we would not bother their clothes. There were hundreds of families that lived in the Mississippi River bottoms then. When the Mississippi River over flowed, the people would have to move to high ground untill the watter went down, these girls were visiting their uncle while the watter had their home flooded.

We went on up the creek to the Hidaway. The two cane poles with the trotline tied to them were going up and down. I got to one cane and Luke got to the other, we pulled the cane out of the bank and back up the bank, pulling the fish up the bank. Luke said we done caught us a heap of catfish. We had six that weighed about three pounds each. We cut some wood and I made a fire in our cook stove.

I was frying the country ham and Luke was cleaning the catfish. I heard some one behind me say gosh that country ham sure do smell good. It was one of the girls that was necked in the creek. They sat on the bench and watched me cook the country ham. I washed the Irish potatoes and sliced them. I put the lard in the skillet and fried the Irish potatoes, by that time Luke had three of the catfish cleaned and washed. I put them in paper sack with the corn meal and the salt and pepper. I put them in the skillet. We just left the catfish in one piece. I cut me a forked willow and trimed the bark off each prong. I used it to turn the fish. I turned them each about three times. When they got golden brown they were done. I used my willow fork to get the fish out of the boiling greese.

One of the girls said we will help you if you will tell us what to do. I was sure they were hungry so I said take that tin buckett and go up the creek to the spring and fill it with watter and bring it back. By the time they got back I had all the fish fried. I gave each of the girls a tin plate with a catfish, a country ham and biscuit and some fried potatoes. One of the catfish was all that Luke and I could eat. The girls ate the too extra. I said "How are you going to pay us for all the food you have eaten?" The oldest girl said "Don't get no funny ideas. We will wash up all of the dishes." I said that will be fine.

Luke and I lay down on our car seats and took us a nap. When we waked up the girls had dumped the greese on the creek bank, they had gotten some sand and taken some willow leaves and cleaned the frying pan, they poured some boiling water in the skillett, it was clean. They had washed all of the tin plates and dried them. They thanked us for the good food and went away happy with a full belly. I am sure it was the best meal they had had since the high watter drove them away from their home.

When I got home that after noon Dill was sitting on Granny's back door steps. He wanted to know how many cat-

33

fish we caught. I told him six. Dill said I have fixed up another trotline. Let's go back down to the creek and set them out. He said "You nose when the birds find that catalfa tree they will eat all the worms up."

It was getting late so we caught the old horse. Dill put his trotline in a sack and got on behind me on the horse. We went back to the creek. It was not any trouble to get the worms. We just drove the horse under the tree and picked them off the leaves. We cut to more cane, and fixed Dills trotline. We baited both trotlines and set them out. It didnt take long and it was a good thing, for Granny was getting worried about us. We got back before it got dark.

The next morning when it was just getting day light, Dill was knocking on my window, he said, "I have already caught the horse and I am ready to go run the trot lines." I slipped into my over alls and put on my tennis shoes. When I went through the kitchen, I looked into the warming clossett on the K stove and got too biscuits and country ham. I put them in a sack with a hand full of cookies I had gotten out of the cookie jar. I gave Dill a country ham and biscuit and half of the cookies. We ate them as we rode the horse down to the creek. After Dill finished the ham and bisket and cookies, Dill would repeat over and over, "I just cant wait to see how manny cat fish we have caught."

When we got to the first trotline and were just starting to raise it, Old Dan the Bull Dog began to growl. Dan always followed us every where we went. I said Dan what are you growling about, just then a voice hollerd out "It is us the girls, call that bull dog back." I called Old Dan and he came back to us. There stood two girls, one with a single barrell shot gun. I said "What are you all doing?" I thought they were squirrell hunting. They said they had spent the knight at the Hideaway. I said were you not scarred to spend the knight out here alone. The bigger girl said "Hell no, anything that had come around last knight would have got a load of shot in its ass." I have no doubt she was telling the truth. That gal was plenty tough.

34

We raised Dill's line and got ten cat fish. Dill got the feed sack we had brought and put the fish into it. He tied a string around the top and placed the sack back in the watter to keep the fish alive. We raised my trotline and it had five fish on it. The girl with the shot gun said "I sure would like to take some fish to Uncle Ben. He has got six kidds and don't have much to eat." I said "You can have my five cat fish and you can bait up the lines and catch some moore." Dill said "I gonna bait my line my self." They went and picked them some worms off the tree. I helped them set out the trotline. When we were finished, I cut a small willow tree with too forks. I peeled the bark off one of the forks. I slipped the peeled fork through the gills and out the mouth of each cat fish. The last I saw of the girls they were on their way to Uncle Ben.

The next day Dill, Luke and I want back to raise Dill's trotline, the catalfa worms were all over the ground, they had eaten all of the leaves off the tree and were on their way to another tree. Dill had eight catfish on his line. He put them in the sack and tied the open end, and placed them in the creek. We went to the Hidaway. I was resting on one of the car seats and Luke was on the other. Dill was laying on the kitchen table. Old Dan started growling, he soon quit when he recognized the girls. Luke said did you all come up her to so some trading. The oldest one said "Hell no, we just came up here to thank Jack for being nice to us. We caught six more cat fish and Uncle Ben had a fish fry. The Mississippi River has gone back in its banks and we are going back home to day." The girls had washed all of the gumbo mud off them, they had clean cut off overalls, and white shirts and they looked real good. I could not help thinking what they were going back to. After the back watter the mosquitoes will be so thick, they will cover you as soon as you go out of the house.

The houses are built on stilts, about ten feet off the ground. At night they will build a small fire with green wood, that is wood that isn't cured out, it will smoke for a long time and that will help keep the mosquitoes away. The worst thing about living in the Mississippi's bottoms, is the drinking

35

watter. You pump a cup and it smells and tasts awful. The old saying is that you tie the hound dog to the pump, when you want a drink of watter, you catch the dog and kiss his ass and then try to drink the watter.

Five years latter when I started to Dyersburg High School, a pretty girl came up to me. She said you don't remember me do you. I said you look kinda familiar. She said do you remember the girls that spent the time, out of back watter with their Uncle Ben. I asked her if she remembered the fish fry on the creek. She said she would never forget it, she said she did not live in the Mississippi bottoms any more. Her father had got a job at textile mill and they lived in mill town. She was on the honor roll in school. Mr. Wheeler was the President of the textile mill, and had the mill give any ones child that worked there and had four years on the honor roll a full scholler ship to the University of Tennessee. Over the thirty years that Mr. Wheeler carried on his schollership program, hundreds of kidds of people that worked at the textile mill finished colledge that would never have been able to go to colledge. He was really a remarkable man.When Peggy finished high school she went to the University of Tennessee and got a degree in education, she came back home and taught in the city schools. She married a lawyer and they have three kidds. Every time we meet, I ask her if she is doing any trading, she laughs and says no. She hugs my neck and we talk about the fish fry on the creek. I say "Girl, you have come a long way from those days." She laughs and says, "Boy you sure got that right."

Golf

There were no swimming pools in Dyersburg at that time. Dyersburg had a 9 hole golf course. The boys in the north end of town all caddied at the golf course, you got 25¢ a round for caddying. Mr. Jack Bratton had a farm on the north end of the course. He had a 10 acre orchard next to the course.

He would tell us we could have all that was on the ground, but please don't shake the trees.

We would hunt balls and play golf every morning. We had one club each.Old man Brady looked after the course. He had a small house at the entrance to the course. He had two iron stakes at the entrance to the course, with a cable going from one to the other. He would lock the cabbles at night so people could not drive over the course.

The town banker would give him a doller on certain nights to leave the cabble unlocked. He and his secretary would meet on the golf course. One night we decided to lock the cable after he had entered. We slipped up close to the banker's car. We each had a pocket full of wallnuts. We let go with a barrage of wallnuts. The banker thought all hell had broke loose. The banker cranked his car in a hurry and started for the entrance to the course. He had left the cable down so all he was going to do was get the hell out of there, so he hit the cabble at a good speed. It made a hell of a rackett. He backed up. By that time old man Brady was up. He came out with his flash light to see what was going on. The banker said "Brady why did you lock me in?" Brady unlocked the cabble and let him out. The banker had to find another place to make love.

High School

I was in the fourth grade when we moved to Dyersburg and went through the 5-6-7 grades in Dyersburg, then went to junior high in the country. I went to senior high in Dyersburg. We had to furnish our own transportation. George Harrison had a car. We paid him $1.00 each a week. We had 4/5 of the basket ball team in the car. Sue H. was 6 ft 2. Neva her sister was 6 ft. Marry Alice and Marry North were small but fast, they played forwards. Seven people in a car made someone have to sit in someone's lap. The first thing they would say, "Give me your hand, I don't want to be pinched all the way to school."

George was 6 ft and weighted 220 lbs. He was really fast. He was stout as a bull. If we had a flat tire on the car he would lift one side of the car and we would place the jack under the axle. We would put the spare tire on and he would lift the car up and we would take the jack out.

The football coach wanted George to try out for football. He put him a full back. I had never played any football. I decided if I was going to have to wait on George to practice, I might as well go out for football too. I didn't weight but 150 lbs. The first game I didn't get to play. I was sub end. George ran over the opisition the first game. He scored 4 TD's. The second game we went to Jackson. They always had the best team in the region. The 3rd play of the game the boy I was sub for got knocked out. I was sent in to replace him. They were playing the single wing. One guard and a half back would come to block the end. By half time they had me bleeding all over. Rocky Palmer was the coach he said "Jack do you think you can stand it for another half?" I didn't anser him but I was sure hoping the guy I was subing for would be able to play.

George played a good game but that night going home he said "This foot ball is rough as hell." The next week Rocky the coach and George had a few words. Rocky said George was not running the play the right way. George said he was. After a few more words, George said he just quit. When George quit I had to quit. I was glad, for I was just not large enough to play football, I have always wondered what George could have done if he and Rocky could have gotten along. He had all of the tools to make a grate player.

Sue H. said "Jack, that girl, Celia, in the big auto has got a crush on you." I said 'I noticed she has been giving me the big eye.' I had noticed she was always parked to watch football practice. That girl was the best thing that happened in my life. I have not known anyone as good as she, and still be a natural person. Ardis Vaughn one of the girls in our class told her she didn't need to date me. She said "He is just plain mean." I guess she was wright.

Rocky P. taught American history. He would take Celia's paper and give her 100 and grade al the other papers by it. Rocky had the last study hall, Celia would go ask him if she could set with me so I could help her with her lessons. He would laugh and say 'go right on, I know he can help you.'

Celia was one person that could get anything that she wanted all of her life. But she never wanted anything. She was always willing to help anyone. She always treated everyone the same. We were married April 16, 1938. I had moved to Memphis. My sister Geneva worked in the office at Western Textile Co. She got me a job as shipping clerk. Celia and I didn't live in Memphis long after we married. We moved back to Dyersburg and I went to work for her father. We sold all the fertilizer that was sold in north west Tennessee. I looked after the fetilizer. We sold natural chillion nitrate and potosh. During the depression people didn't use any fertilizer, some people would use it one year and make a big yield. And not use it the next, the yield would be way down. They would think the fertilizer had hurt their land.

My first son was born a year and a day after Pearl Harbor.

PART II

THE WAR

Jack, Picadilly, London, 1943

Jack and Friends,
Buckingham Palace, 1944

Jack with Murray, 1943

The War

I was drafted into the army in early 1943 and passed my physical for the army, navy and marines. At that time you could not be drafted into the navy and marines, and I thought I would get to be with my wife and baby longer if I chose the army, so I waited to be drafted. I was assigned to the M.P.s (Military Police.) We rode trains most of the time.

One night I was riding a train from Chicago to Pittsburg. I was on duty with a big boy from the mountains of East Tennessee. He was about 6 ft 6 and weighed about 250 lbs. Our job was to keep order on the train. At each station the ladies of the volunteer group would bring cookies and sandwiches to the train for the soldiers. We would destribute them. On one trip a little parritrooper on the train had had a few drinks. He wanted to take off his clothes. The train had women and children on them. Each time we come through the coach we would have to make him put his clothes on. Big Dempsy said we will get rid of him at the next stop. The next stop was small place. Dempsy grabbed the soldier and got his duffell bag. He carried the soldier to the side of the track and I carried his bag. Big Dempsy said "You little bastard, pull your clothes off if you want to." We deposited him there. I hope he made it. It was cold outside. I don't think it was long before he sobbered up.

On Christmas Day, we left Camp Shanks N.Y. We went down the Hudson River. We had been at sea for 2 days when we got our last mail call. I was sitting on the deck reading my mail. J.C. Bain and William Hampton were the only two men on the boat from my hometown. J.C. Bain come to where I was sitting, he wanted to show me his letter from his wife. She wanted a divorce. He said "What would you do?" I said "I would just go jump overboard." He said "You are crazzy." He had just left when William Hampton come and set down beside me. He had a letter from his wife. She wanted a divorce. She was in love with an air force officer at the air base. I had one more letter to open from my wife. I said "I don't know whether to open it or not." But I was not worried. I was sure I had married an angel.

I was stationed on the bay outside of Weymouth England, I was attached to a tank retreiver company. They were taking care of the camp. Their job was to run the kitchens and handle the security. Our job was to meet the convoys and get them to the right spot in the camp. The camp was in a woods over looking the bay. The first troops to arrive were the 1st and 4th Infantry Divisions. They had been in combat in Africa and they were batttle hardened. The first thing they did was dig them a fox hole. We didn't think we needed one, untill the Germans bombed us that night. We were trying to scratch one with our hands. The German air force was pretty weak by then.

We were on top of a big bluff. The invasion fleet was in the bay below. The whole area was ringed with antiaircraft artillery and with all of the fire power on the ships in the bay the German planes had an impossible job to get to the invasion fleet, they carried block buster bombs. They would try to bomb the ships, but would end up dropping their bombs in the woods on us. The German plane sounded like a dog growling. You could tell one as soon as you heard it. The planes would arrive at 12 o'clock each night. There were a few men killed by the bombing. We lost 4 out of my outfit. It was mostly nuisance raids. It caused us to loose some sleep.

We had three invasion manuvers. We would load the L.S.T.'s with troops, they would take them around to lands end and they would hit the beach. On the last manuver the British Escorts left the L.S.T.'s too early. The German U. boats slipped in and torpetoed the L.S.T.'s. They then dropped depth charges. The concussion killed the men in the water. I do not know how many soldiers were killed, but trucks took them off the boats. They were stacked like cord wood. This lasted for several days. I do not know where they carried them but I read later about this English lady seeing all those American soldiers' corpses stacked in a field. The security was so tight I am sure they were buried in the invasion area.

A Letter from Jack to Geneva

Dear Geneva,

I got your letter saying that [our brother] Bill has finished High School and has passed all of his exams for the air force. He has already reported to Kiesler Field, Mississippi as an air caddett. I sure hope every thing works well for him. I know that Moma is heart broken to see her baby going to war.

I have been stationed in London for the past four months. I am now on detached service. I am attached to a tank retreiver out fit, they are running the invasion camp. Our job is to meet the convoys in the staging area and bring them to areas they are assigned to. There they will wait their turn. I have my Jeep. I get my orders from my officers, but I eat and sleep with the tank retriever out fit. We are camped in a woods on a cliff over looking Weymouth Bay. All of the invasion fleet is ancored in the bay. The Germans try to bomb the ships in the bay every night. With all of the antiaircraft guns on the cliff and all of the guns on the ship, the German planes end up dropping their bombs on the troops in the surrounding woods.

We got an order to come to the rail head and pick up too hundred and sixty new Harley Davidson mortorsickles. We have never had any mortorsickle training. It rains a little each day over here and the roads are always slick. Most of the convoys are tanks or half tracks. You just make one slip and mortorsickle and rider are gone. We have lost a lott of mortorsickles and riders. I still can't understand why we were not given mortorsickle training before we came over seas. There was a young boy, Mark McCuller. I tried to talk him out of taking a mortorsickle. He would not listen to me. He said he had not ridden a mortorsickle but three or four times. He lasted four days doing convoy work. He slipped in front of a half track. It crushed him and the mortorsickle.

This part of England is covered with army equipment and men. We had a tent on a small square in the middle of Weymouth England. That was where we waited to get our orders. We gave away surplus tea for a couple of days and we *had the square lined with people wanting tea. It was going to rot in the woods, but the captain came by and saw all of the people lined up waiting for free tea. He said "What the hell is going on here?" I explained to him about the tea going to waste. He said "Don't bring any more. We will have the hole town down here waiting in line for free tea." It really hurt me to see all of that tea going to waste because the American soldier does not drink tea.*

I have looked at thousands of faces over the last few weeks but I have not seen one person that I new. The soldiers all look alike.

We moved the Free French Army into the camp area two days ago. That is the wildest bunch of soldiers I have ever seen. They have run over several of their own men. One soldier in a tank set off a burst of machinegun fire down a row of his men. He killed four or five. I saw General Degoul looking them over. You can spot him easily for he is ten inches taller than every one else. I don't get close to where they are camped. You can't tell what they are going to do.

Love,

Jack

No one was supposed to leave the camp but the M.P.s. We had a tent on a small square in the middle of Weymouth. We would get our instructions on where to go from there.

One day I was about to go to Weymouth, one soldier in the tank outfit that I was attached to asked if he could go to Weymouth with me. I was not supposed to let him go but I did. When we returned we were walking through the woods by the cook tent. The soldier that had gone to Weymouth with me stopped to talk to the soldier that was on guard in front of the cook tent. He said "I have just got back from town." The guard was in the same company as the one that had gone to town with me. I did not know their names. The guard said "I know you are lying you can't get out of this camp." He took his carbine off his shoulder and placed the barrel in the middle of the other soldier's chest. The gun went off, the soldier said "You shot me." He started going down. We caught him and layed him down on the ground. The last words he said were "You killed me." I always wondered if there had been bad blood between them. I had to go to South Hampton to a general court marshall for the soldier that did the shooting. I told the court the way I saw the incendent. I do not know what the outcome was for the soldier.

Three or four times each day a call would come over the loud speaker to call the father. Someone had shot themselves. The men that had been through 3 invasions were dreading this one. The day of the invasion I was on Portland Bill, this is a peninsula out in the Channell. I have never seen so many planes. They went in a steady stream for 12 hrs. First the B17 bombers, the C46 pulling gliders, the C46 cargo planes loaded with parratroopers. We were busy moving troops from then on. The next day a B17 came back shot up bad, all of the crew had bailed out over the bay. The pilot and co-pilot stayed with the plane and crashed landed it about 50 yards from the shore. They got out and waded to shore. I think the rest of the crew drowned.

A Letter from Dill to Granny

Dear Granny:

I am writing to tell you I have been drafted into the Army. I am stationed at Fort Orglethrope, Georgia. I think of all the good times we had, when Jack and I were boys. I think of all the rainy days, when we did not go to school. We would have spelling bees. The one that got the most words spelled right, got the first popcorn ball. We always popped a dishpan full of popcorn. You would melt butter and sorgum molasses and pour them over the popcorn and roll the popcorn into balls. I also remember that Cindy always got the first popcorn ball. I remember that you always made us write a note for anything we wanted. If I wanted a cookie, I would have to write a note, saying, "Granny I sure would like to have one of your cookies." All of the words had to be spelled correctly.

I remember when we would play domanoes, you would always make us take our turns keeping the score. I remember how Cindy would watch Jack and I to see that we did not make a mistake in keeping the score. She had an eye like a hawk. You and Cindy won most of the games. You used to give us arithmatic problems on the black board. Cindy would always get hers finished first. She would set and watch to see if we made a mistake.

You would always tell me, Dill look every one strait in the eye when you talk to them. There will be things you won't know, but if you look them in the eye, they will think you know.

Granny, my officers are all white. My captain was raised on a farm in north Georgia. He and I get along real well. He called me in his office when I first got there. I soluted him and said I was Private Dillworth Day. He said "Private Day I have been watching you. You are now Sargent Dillworth Day. I am sending you to the non commishion oficer school. I want you to try hard. I want you to watch all the other men I send to the school." When we finished the school, I reported to the captain. I said "Sargent Dillworth Day reporting sir." He said "No you are now First Sargent Dillworth Day. I am putting you in charge. I want you to tell me who you would like to have for a company clerk." I said that Private Tom Clark has finished high school and had some college work. He said "Call him in." I called Tom Clark in, he soluted the captain and said "Private Tom Clark reporting sir." The Captain pitched him some stripes and said "You are now Staff Sargent Tom Clark. You will be working with First Sargent Day. I think you will do a good job."

He called in Privates Johnson, Smith and Moore. He gave them their stripes and said, "You are now platoon sargents, each of you will be over a platoon. I want you to keep strick disapline. If any one gives you any trouble, you bring him before me, and I will set him strait. I want you to take them on a four mile hike each morning. You will hike ninety minutes and rest ten. During the morning and afternoon you will give too

48

hours of close order drill. Be sure that they make their beds and clean their quarters every day."

The captain said "Sargent Dill, why do you take the four hour drill every day?" I said "Captain, I was raised on a farm, I am used to working and I don't want the men to think I cant do any thing they can do. It is rough on these men that were raised in the cities. When I holler 'on your feet' after the ten minutes rest, they can't do much complaining for I am the first one on his feet."

Granny I think of you and home all of the time. If it wasn't for you, I would not be the first sargent of this company. You taught me all I learned in school, on the rainy days. The thing that amazes me is that you made it so much fun. Cindy wrote me and said that she is working at Milan Arsinell. The arnisell is twenty miles from home. There is a buss that takes workers to the arsinell each day. Cindy is making a lott of money. She has had our house wired. The T.V.A. ran its line to our house last year. She has bought Moma an electric cook stove, a refrigerator and a washing machine. Moma just can't believe it. She thinks she has died and gone to heaven. I sure am glad to know that she won't have to stand over that hot wood burning cook stove any more. I remember how hot she would get in the summer, cooking a meal for all of us. She won't have to bend over the wash board and wash all the clothes. That used to take her one day each week.

We never did have ice in the summer. The left over food was always given to the hogs or chickens. It sure is going to make a big change in her life. I know Paw is glad he does not have to cut wood for the cook stove every day.

Granny don't forget to write to me. There is nothing that makes me feel as good as getting a letter from home. I always feel let down when we have mail call, and I don't get a letter. I make it fine during the day when I am bussy, but when the sun goes down, I really get lonesome for home. I know that Jack must get lonesome for his wife and baby. I know he has already shipped over seas. I think Cindy said he was in En-

gland. We are about finished with our training. I am sure we will be shipping over seas before long. Cindy saved her money and bought the small farm that our moma and daddy lived on. She also saved enough to go to Lane Colledge. She will major in education. I know she will make a good teacher.

Dill

A Letter from Granny to Jack

Dear Jack,

I hope this letter will find you safe and sound. I think of you and all of the boys that have gone off to war. I say a prayer for you all every night. I know you must be lonesome for your wife and baby. There has been four boys in the comunity missing in action. I really greive for their families. I just pray that you and Dill will make it home safely. I had a letter from Dill the other day. He said that he had finished his training and he is expecting to be shipped over seas before long. He has your address and he is going to get in touch with you.

There is just no way to tell you how nice it is to have electricity in our house. We have bought a radio, and we always listen to the war news. I have a new electric range. I have moved the old wood stove to the barn. My new stove has every thing on it. I has two ovens and a clock. I have a new refrigerator, and a washing machine. We have a new hot water heater and are building a new bath room. It is grand to have hot watter all of the time.

The weather has begun to get warm. We did not have a cold winter. I look for the bugs to be bad in my garden. We did not have enough cold weather to freeze them out. I can hardley wait to start a new garden. We have already planted an Irish potato patch, and a patch of sweet corn. I have also planted my onions and cabbage. My arthritis makes it hard for me to garden, but I crawl around and do my best. I sure do enjoy raising a garden.

Love,

Granny

I had been on the look out for Dill's outfit. I was driving by a convoy and I saw the number of his outfit. Later that day I found where he was located in the woods. I checked and found his tent. He was in the comand tent. I walked in and said "Watch that goat!" I always said that to watch him jump. He was really glad to see me. Dill was 1st sargent of the company. I asked Dill how he got to be 1st sargent. He said "Granny got it for me. She taught me to read and wright and my math. The best thing she taught me was to look everyone strait in the eye and say yes sir and thank you."

We told his captain about our times on the farm, about the goat, Old Dan and the bull. He had a big laugh. That night the Germans bombed us again. One of the bombs fell on the tent where Dill was sleeping. He and six of his men were killed.

A Letter from Jack to Granny

Dear Granny,

I am writing you some real bad news. I had been watching for Dill's out fit for days. I new he was in a trucking out fit. I had his out fits number. I spotted it and got to talk to him for a few minutes. I told him I would be over the see him when I finished my last convoy for the day. He and his captain were in their headquarters tent. His captain got a big laugh when we told him about our fishing and hunting. We told him about old Dan and how he would catch the goat. We told him about the big fish and how old man Bob tired to catch his mate. We really did have a lotts of good laughs. We told him about how the goat would slip up behind you and but you in the back.

I left their tent about twelve o'clock. We usually get bombed about twelve o'clock each night. I know that they did not have time to dig a fox hole. I had just gotten to my tent when I heard the first wave of bombers. I ran to my fox hole and dived in. The Germans were using the largest bombs, they were trying to bomb the invasion fleet in the bay. I know that Dill did not have a fox hole, but it did not help one of the boys in my outfit. He was in a fox hole and a bomb fell close by, a piece of shrapnel went through the ground fifty feet and went through his helmet. He was the only man that we lost. I went to check on Dill the next day. A bomb fell on their tent. It killed Dill and six more men in his outfit. I sure am glad I got to spend those last few hours with Dill.

I dont know how many soldiers were killed in the raid, but I am sure there were manny more. The Germans must not have many bombers left, for we dont see but ten or twelve each night, and they always loose some if they get close to the ships in the bay. I dont see how any get past all those shells exploding at one time. I know that the invasion cant be far away. This hole area is covered with men and equipment.

I really feel for the men in the first and fourth infantry divisions. They are in the camp with me, they have been through three invasions, and they know just how rough it is going to be. The other men that have not seen combat are just wondering what it will be like.

Love,

Jack

After the beach head and a ship port were secured we were not needed for convoy work anymore and were sent back to London.

We were in London but one day when the buzzy bombs started coming in. The first day their was only 2. But after that they were coming in at all times, day and knight. You could hear them for a long distance. But there was no danger until the moter cut off. The poor tenoment districks were the hardest hit. The poor people would take all their family to the underground railway stations at knight. They would take a blanket and sleep on the concreet. I was billited in an old hotell at 101 Picadilly across Green Park from Bucking Ham Palace. We had an alarm siren that would go off when a buzzy bomb was near. I awoke one knight and the siren was going full blast. I was on the 6th floor. I got my flash light but I heard the motor on the buzzy bomb cut out. I knew I didn't have time to get any place. I remember I got my pillow and pulled it over my head. The buzzy bumb fell in Green Park. It blew all the windows out of the building, but it did not hurt anyone.

I was working at the American Embasy on Grovner Square. We were the security for the embasy. We had to wear white gloves, white belts and white hats. I felt like a monky instead of a soldier.

I remember when 4 or 5 rocketts hit London. I was at 101 Picadilly about 4 o'clock one afternoon when a rockett hit one block from Grovners Square. The pub was in a 6 story building. There was a hole in the ground 30 ft deep. Just past the corner on the street where the rockett hit were 4 sailors. The glass had cut them up, they were all dead.

One day I was driving a jeep in the east end of London, I heard someone hollering from an air raid shelter. He was calling "M.P. come here." When I got to the shelter he was standing there with just his shirt on. He was in the air force and was on leave to London. He had taken a girl to the air raid shelter and when he pulled off his pants she had grabed them and run off with them. I ask him how long he had been waiting, he said about 4 hours. He said "I never thought I would be this glad to see an M.P." I had an old blanket in the jeep. He covered up with it and I carried him to the Red Cross building where he was staying. He rapped the blankett around him and went up to his room and got some more pants. He brought my blankett down and thanked me for helping him.

A Letter from Jack to Granny

Dear Granny,

I am stationed in London, England. I live at 101 Pickadilly. I am just one block from Pickadilly Circle. Green Park is in front of where I live. You walk across Green Park to Bucking Ham Palace. This town has been bombed every day for years. The poor people have suffered so much and are still suffering. You dont see many fat people over here, they just don't have much to eat.

Every thing is blacked out over hear at night. They have a black out curtain at every door. We drive around at night with black out lights. It is about like driving with two small flash lights. We don't have many wrecks, for there is not but a very few driving at night. Most of the people are in air raid shelters or where they can get to one. The Germans have turned their newest bomb on London. We call it a buzzy bomb. It is a small air plane loaded with high explosives. They just put the right amount of fuel to reach London, and when the fuel runs out the bomb goes down. It sure is a funny feeling when you hear one coming, and then you hear it start sputtering and you know it is running out of fuel and the bomb is on its way down.

The buzzy bombs did the most damage in the tenament districks. The houses were all joined together. One buzzy bomb would level a row of houses. The poor people would be running and screaming. If it was in the day time they would help put out the fires and try to find some of their belongings. I sure did feel sorry for those poor people. The buzzy bomb did not have to much effect, militarily. It was just an extra hardship on the people. The poor people had been spending the night in the underground rail station for years. They would each take a blanket and sleep on the floor next to the tracks. I don't see how they got much sleep. I guess you eventually get used to all the noise.

Love,

Jack

It was the day before Xmas, 1944 when I got to barricks from working at the embasy. I was told to go look at the bulliten board. It said these men are now rifle replacements in the infantry. My name was on it. We had one week before we had to report. We were being replaced by men that were not fit for combat. I said I was not going to work that week. I reported back in time to go to the replacement camp.

The replacement camp was in South England. When we got there, there was just one officer to meet us. He said he was supposed to give us infantry training. He didn't have a M1 rifle. His orders were to send so many men to the front every 4 weeks. We were the second group to arrive. The first were medics. The medics had never had any infantry training. I remember what the captain told them. He said "I did not have anything to train you with, but if you can last 3 days at the front you will get your training.'" They went to the front and didn't know how to load a M1 riffle.

The captain gave us lectures each day. That was all the training we got.

A Letter from Geneva to Jack

Dear Jack,

I am writing to tell about Aunt Molly Wynn. She has been sick for about three months. Her sister, Lizzy, is looking after her. We carried her her favorite chockolate cake. Dr. Hall came to see he while we were there. He checked her over and kidded her. He asked her when she was going to get out of bed and start picking her cotton. She laughed and said loudy, "I don't spect I will ever pick any more cotton." When Dr. Hall got ready to leave, I followed him out side and asked him how Aunt Molly was doing. He said "She is getting weaker at each visit." He said "When you get ready to be ninety two, it's hard for you to gain strength after an illness."

Aunt Molly asked us about everyone in the neighborhood. She asked about all of the boys that have gone off to war. She said she says a prayer for them all each night. We stayed a long time. When we got ready to leave we held her hand and said a prayer and all cried. Lizzy followed us out side and thanked us for coming. When we left we knew we would probably never see Aunt Molly alive again.

The next week Gran Smith, Aunt Molly's cousin, came to our house to tell us that Aunt Molly had passed away. The whole neighborhood was sad. Every one had the same thing to say about Aunt Molly. She loved every body, black or white, and every one that came in contact with Aunt Molly loved her.

There was a box placed on the counter of the Farmers Supply Company. Every one put some money in the box for Aunt Molly. There was enough to pay for all the funeral, and enough to buy a nice marker for her grave. The enscryption on the tomb stone read "Aunt Molly Wynn, died age 92. She loved every body and every body loved her." We all went to the funeral. Her church was small, there were so many people they could not start to get into the church. The women sat in the church and the men stood out side, there were as many white as their were black. The preacher said "I am just going to say a prayer for Aunt Molly. I want anyone that has any thing to say to come down." Granny and I went down together and said all the nice things that Aunt Molly had done for the community. Granny said a short piece. She said "Aunt Molly I know you are in heaven, if you are not there, none of us have a chance." The people were going down for two hours. It was not a dry eye in the church. Every one's family was Aunt Molly's family. She had no children of her own but she thought of every one as her family.

I can see her now when she would come by the house to see Granny. If it was in the summer time Granny and Aunt Molly would set on the back porch, in rocking chairs. Granny would fix two glasses of ice tea. If she had Aunt Molly's favorite chockolite cake, they would have ice tea and cake. If she did not have cake, she always had cookies in the cooky jar.

Aunt Molly was the first person to see most of the young people in the neighborhood. She would come to the house a *day or too before a baby was supposed to arrive. If Dr. Hall was not able to arrive in time Aunt Molly would deliver the baby. In the winter, the road would get empassible. It was nice to know that Aunt Molly was there.*

There was not much cash money available, Aunt Molly would stay a day or too after the baby came. When she got ready to go home, the man of the house would ask her what she needed. He would load the car with a sack of Irish potatoes, and a country ham. Aunt Molly did not need to raise a large garden. Every place she stopped, she would be given something. It was a way of thanking her for all she did for everyone. Dr. Hall never charged her for a sick call. He alway thought he was in her debt. Dr. Hall did not have to make manny calls to Aunt Molly. Every one marvelled at how Aunt Molly could be around so manny sick people and never get sick her self.

I will write again soon. Take care.

Love,

Geneva

I tried to volinteer in the armored division. They needed some M.P.'s but they didn't have time to process my records. It was probably a good thing. The armored division would leave the M.P.'s at intersections to direct traffic. They were fair game for snipers. That would leave no one to show the rest of the column the right way to go.

I went across the channell in an L.S.T. filled with replacements for I Company, 120th Infantry. (That company earlier lost all but 5 men at St. Low. The smoke screen over the German line was to mark where the American planes were to bomb. The wind shifted and the 2nd wave bombed their own men. This was before I joined the outfit. The 30th Division spearheaded the 7th Army all the way across Europe. They made the breakthrough at St. Low, the Germans saw the Old Hickory Patch on their sleeves with OH and XXX and they called them Roosevelt's S.S. troops.

Some one was way off base in the chain of supplies. They had no winter clothes for replacements in the pipe line. After the Germans made their charge at the battle of the Bulge there were infantry companies with only 15 & 20 men in a company. The Germans made their spear head at a spot where the 106th Infantry Division had just gone in the line. The 106th had just been over seas a short time. The 28th Division was on one flank and the 90th on the other. They were battle hardened and they held good. But the 106th lost over half of their men the first 3 days.

The Germans were not the worst enemy. The weather was awfull. The men were so cold. It is impossible to explain how miserable everyone was. I had old rough leather boots. They were full of water most of the time. The Germans had it fine untill the weather cleared and the fighter bombers got on their tail. After that roads were covered with burned out German equipment.

There was a building on the outskirts of Maly Belgium. It was used as an aid station. It was the first place you went with frost bite and frozzen feet. It had a trap door that could be let down from inside, it was like a farmer's corn cribb where you let the door down to scoop the corn in. The soldiers that had gan green already started, had to have their feet amputated there. They would amputate the feet, put a tag on them, and drop them out the trap door. It was a great relief when they looked at your feet and said you could make it to the hospital.

In the hospital wards 95 percent of the patients had frost bite or frozzen feet. You could not stand to have a sheet on your feet it hurt so bad. All you could see down the row of beds were big toes about half the size of a coffee cup. You could not stand any weight on them. We were in the ward for about three weeks before the swelling went down and we could put our weight on our feet. When we got to where we could stand our weight on our feet, we were sent to the rehab. That is where they get you in shape physically to go back to the front. They would take you for a hike each day. They could not force you to walk if it made your feet swell. Some soldiers would stomp on their feet to make them swell. If you got to where you could walk pretty good you were on your way back to the front. By the time I went through the hospital and rehab and got back to my outfit the war was all but over.

We were waiting for the Rushians to take Berlin when the war in Europe ended. We were sent to occupy Mannnheim, Germany. We entered the city at 12 p.m. The Germans were scared to death. I suppose they thought we were going to treat them like the S.S. had treated the people they occupied.

The only houses left were on the outskirts. My squad took a house with 2 stories and a basement. It was a nice home with carpets 2 inches thick on the floors. There was a woman about 40 and a girl 15, a man about 70 and a boy about 12. We let the man and the boy go to the attick and the woman and girl go to the basement. We went to bed in their beds. The next morning the woman gathered all of our dirty clothes and carried them to the basement and washed them. I gave her a bar of soap. Soap was like gold to them. The woman went to the basement and came back with a pitcher of snops. One of the men in my squad said "Jack give her another bar of soap, and tell her more snops." I did and he watched where she got it. From then on we got the snops when we wanted it.

The woman was real nice, she ask me to get her the coffee grounds at the kitchen when we were through with them. She said she had not had a cup of coffee in 4 years. I got her the coffee grounds. I also slipped a package of fresh coffee under my coat for her. She was really gratefull, we were not supposed to fratonize with the Germans, but we did not pay it any mind. You could not live in the house with people and not talk to them.

We searched all of the house for guns and amo. We found a mortor scuter or a mortorsickle in the most of the atticks. We had captured a salt mine that was full of wine, snops, beer and conyock. We would send a truck to the mine and load it with all the mixture. We moved out of the homes after we cleaned up an old German barricks.

There were about 200 girls from the Balken states that had been brought in by the Germans to work on the farms. After the war they had no place to go. We put a fence around an old calvery barricks. We gave them some cots and blanketts. We gave then a cook stove and tables. We brought them rations. One girl from Poland told me she and her sister were on their way to church one Sunday. She said a German army truck stoped and picked them up. She said the German farmers were good to them as long as they did their work. We had to send guards down to them. It was mostly to keep the G.I.'s out.

We had started training the new replacements, all the old men were being sent home. We were getting ready to go to the invasion of Japan. We were told to expect one million casualties.

A Letter from Jack to Geneva

Dear Geneva,

Mama wrote me about Grandady passing away. I guess all the fish in the Forked Deer River will have a holloday. He realy did enjoy going fishing. He and Granny are in their ninetys. I suppose you are alloted so many miles and when you run your course, that the motor just stops. I do not look for Granny to live very long after he has passed away. She has spent her life waiting on him.

For the last few months we have been in occupation in Germany. We are now moved to the coast and are getting ready to go to Japan. The men with enough points have been sent home. They sure do deserve to be sent home, this division has spear headed the Seventh Army all across Germany. We are getting new replacements, the training is just as close to combat as is possible. We are using all live ammunition. They are expecting ten percent causulties in training, with raw recruits and live ammunitions. We are having casulties every day. They are expecting one million casulties on the envasion of Japan. I sure hope we come through the United States on our way to Japan, but I have heard that we are going strait from here to Japan.

I have heard that some divisions have already left for Japan. You hear a lott of rummers and you never know what to believe. I got a letter from Moma and she says Bill is on a B-17 bomber. I wonder if he will take any of his training at the Dyersburg air base. I think that is the last training before combat. I have run into some air force men over here and they never want to go back there. They lost so many planes there because of the foggy weather.

Another Letter to Geneva

Dear Geneva:

All hell broke loose the other day. We got the news that the second attomic bomb had been dropped on Japan and the war in the Pacific was over. All training stopped, and every one celebrated There is no way to describe the feeling. I really feel like I have a chance to see my family again. Before, you just didn't want to think about it. It is really sad to think of all the good men that have been lost and will never get to see their families again.

We pitched one hell of a party, and it has been going on for three days. I think that I will be in the next group to go home. I am sure they will keep the young replacements over here in occupation. The last German troops we captured were boys twelve to fourteen and old men sixty to seventy. I am sure the German mothers will be glad to see their babys come home.

I got my papers today, I am to be attached to an antiaircraft battery. I am to report to Rheems France, to wait for them to get ready to go home. Rheems is about twenty miles from Paris.

I don't know how long I will have to wait. The antiaircraft battery is guarding the war crimes trials. They are guarding

Himmler, Gobles, Herman Gering and all of the other big wheels in the Hitler's high command. I visited the Rheems Cathedral, it is one of the most beautiful cathedrals in all of Europe. I wonder how it has gone through all the wars and never been touched.

I am leaving tomorrow to go to the United States maximum security prison. The antiaircraft battery that I am going home with is doing guard duty there. All they have left is the prisiners that have the death sentence. They take out so manny each day. They have a long trailer truck with wire cages built on it, they fill the truck twice each day and take them to the spot where they are hanged by the neck. One of the prisoners that I have talked to is an American Indian, they call him Big Chief. He was in an artillary battery, he made it through the war in Europe. When the war ended he went A.W.O.L., stayed drunk for four days. He came back to his outfit in the middle of the night. He found his riffle and shot his first sargent. When they tried Big Chief for shooting his first sargent, they ask him why he did it. All he would tell them was, "He snored, I couldn't sleep." I visited Big Chief before they put him into the wire cage on the truck. I ask him if had a message for his folks back home. All he say was "Hell no, hell no." I waved to him after they loaded him on the truck. He did not wave back. His expression never did change.

They will have this prison empty in three more days. We will go to Antwerpt Belgium to get the boat for home. I still have my bag of French franks. I guess I will be able to convert some of them into American dollars. It has been almost a year since I was sent to the infantry. I have moved so much in this year it just doesn't seem real.

The men going to the hang man for the last too days have been black. Most of them were framed by the French. Hoars said they were raped, but I dont think it was so, there is no way to rape a French hoar. The soldiers would not pay and they hollered rape to get even. We arrived at the port of Antwerpt the 10th of December. We are going home on the Victory Ship Elnora Gay. We are supposed to be home and discharged before Xmas.

The happiest day of my life was the day I heard the Japs had surrendered. I was sent back to Rheims France to wait my turn to go home. We were on the Shampain Plains. You could go to Parris every day. The young G.I.'s that were waiting to go in occupation would go to Paris every day. They would take discarded clothes to Paris and sell them. They would get $40 for a pair of boots, $60 for an overcoat, $10 for a bar of soap, $50 for a carton of sigerettes. They would usually return about 12 p.m. and start a poker game.

I would go to bed at 5 o'clock and get me a few hours sleep. I knew they would wake me when they came in. Most of them would be full of wine and conyack. It was no trouble to beat them at poker. I had a bag full of French franks. At that time you could go to the army post ofice and buy mony orders. At last the Army put a stop to buying mony orders. When we got to the boat in Brussels Belgum to come home the pay master would let you exchange $400 in French franks for American dollars, most of the soldiers were broke. I would give them 400 in French franks and they would give me 200 in dollars, they were glad to do it. For it gave them $200 where they would have had nothing.

Antwerpt, Belgium Dec. 11, 1945. We boarded the Victory Ship. We were told we would be home and discharged before Xmas. We had been at sea for 3 days when the weather turned bad. On the 4th day it was getting pretty rough. On the 5th day the waves looked like mountains coming at you. Some ships were already giving out distress calls. By this time the ship had been closed up so you could not see out. You could not walk if you did not have something to hold on to.

I found a door open to the cold storage locker. I got me 2 dozen oranges and hid them in my bag. I never did get sea sick. I credit the oranges for keeping me from getting sick. Some of the soldiers were so sick they looked green. They had vomited on the floor so much it was slick as ice.

For the next 48 hours every time the ship rolled I thought that this is it. I was sure it was going under. I was in the bow and each time the ship rolled, the ancor would hit the side of the ship. I was just sure it was going to knock a hole in the ship. When we would get on the crest of a wave the propeller would get out of the watter. The ship would quiver so hard. I was sure it was going to break in too. We had twice the amount of soldiers on board as the ship usually carried. We were blown so far north that if we had sunk and someone had been lucky enough to get in a life boat he would have frozen to death in a few minutes. I was so scared I was numb. I knew our only chance was for the boat to stay afloat. I had read about Henry Kizzers victory ships, breaking in too. All I could think of was that after all I had been through I was going to get killed on my way home. I thought when I was sent to the infantry as a replacement that I had made a bad choice when I did not take the navy. But I changed my mind about the navy after this storm.

We made port in St. Johns Newfoundland on Xmas Eve. It looked like one huge mountain of ice. I think if they would have let me, I would have spent the rest of the winter in Newfoundland. When we got off the boat the captain gave each one of us a ship's paper. He said that he had been at sea for 23 years and this was by far the worst storm he had ever been in. He said that for 48 hours, each time the ship rolled he thought it was going to sink. I kneeled down and kissed the gang plank when I left the ship. The Victory ship Elnora Gay had brought me home safely.

Jack and Murray combining beans

PART III

AFTER THE WAR

Jack with grandson Mac

Jack and J.R., duck hunters

Duncan, Mac, Jack and Fish

Return

My wife and I had 100A of land and during the war we rented our house furnished to a doctor on the air base. My wife moved in with her father and mother while I was in the army. I had saved enough from the army to buy a 340 A farm after the war. I rented it for a 1/4 share of the crop. I had saved me some money and I went into farming with my father-in-law and brother-in-law. We raised 800 A cotton, 600 A soy beans and 600 A corn.

We had 26 houses on the farm. We furnished each family with a house and all the truck patch they wanted. We furnished a milk cow to each family that wanted one. We paid on hourly wages. We had 50 mules and 2 tractors. In 1947 the tractors were not large. We used the tractors to disk and bed the land. We cultivated with the mules. We had 300 Hereford cows. We raised 50 A alfalfa for hay.

In the 1940's most of the fertilizer came in 100 lb. sacks. We would mix potosh and natural chillian nitrate on a truck and drill it in the top of the row. We did not have any chemicals for grass or weeds. All we had was a plow and a hoe. When the cotton got about 2 inches high, we would thin it to 2 stalks in each hill.

It was my job to stay with the cotton choppers who cut the weeds with hoes. I would fill a 50 gal. tank with watter for drinking and put 50 lbs. of ice in it. I had a boy to carry the watter around to the choppers. We would start at 6 a.m. and chop until 9 a.m. Then we would sit down and rest for 15 min. I would file all the hoes before we started. We would chop until 11:30. I had a truck to pick everyone up and take them home for lunch. We would pick them up at 1 p.m. and we would chop until 3 p.m. We would rest 15 min. then chop until 6 p.m. We did this all of the summer. We had to chop the cotton 3 times.

Tenants

All of the families on the farm were white. All had owned small farms in North Alabama and Mississippi. The land was very poor there. It was rocky and hilly but they had always eaked out a living. Their cash crop was cotton. In the early 1930's the boll weavell arrived in that part of the country. It completely wiped out their main cash crop.

The first families to migrate to our farm were the Stutts and Phillipps. Then came the Canadas, Heppses, Williamses, Hineses, McGloglans, Littles, Prathers, Pannells, Hills. All of these people were used to hard work. The land that their fathers had settled on was so poor it was a grind just to feed and cloth your family. They were all hard working good people. When the cotton picker was invented, I wondered what they would do. Most of them migrated to cities. Some went to Gary, Indiana, some to Memphis, but most went to Chicago, Ill.

The women on the farm in those days were the ones that did the hardest work. It was a saying that the man on the farm worked from sun to sun, but the woman's work was never done. They would get up at 4 a.m., cook the noon meal, then cook breakfast for the family, do field work until noon, fix lunch, then go back to the field and work untill 6 p.m. It was the same rutine each day. On the day that it rained, she would wash and iron the cloths for the family. Most of the women had rather be in the field. They would leave one of the older girls with the younger kidds.

We would all keep together in the field. Someone was always telling a tale. The men were talking hunting and fishing. The women were talking gardening or the church. I was bussy chopping on the kidds rows. I didn't want them to get to far behind.

After my brother-in-law and I divided the land, I had 15 houses and got 300 A cleared land and 600 A of woods and swamp. I just needed 3 men. The older people lived on in the houses rent free. They raised a garden. Their utility bill was just $1 per month.

Clearing the Land

The politicions had talked about snagging the river for 20 years. They finally got around to doing it. It gave me good drainage, for my land had been catching sediment for 50 years. All I had to do was clear the land and dig drainage ditches to the river.

Most of the hardwood trees had been killed by watter standing on them. The buck brush and maple and sypress were easy to clear. I would hire a man with a clearing blade and dozer. He would cut the trees, push them in wind rows and set them on fire. It was my job to pick up the chunks. I would clear about 75 A each year.

I had a groham chissell plow. I would take the plows off the tines and move all the tines on the back bar. I would go down the burn rows and rake the tree chunks in piles. That made it easier to pick up the chunks. I would put the plows back on the tines and chissell plow the land. I would drill the soy beans and roll the ground. I rolled the chunks that were left back in the ground so the combine would not pick them up. The yield was good on the fresh made soil. Each year when you chisselled the land you would have to pick up the chunks. It would take 3-4 years for a stump to rot out.

I had 3 sons and they all hated picking up chunks. Russell the youngest hated picking up chunks worse than Jack, Jr. or Murray, who farmed with me later. When he started to high school, he would always "need" to take some extra courses in the summer school. He was real smart in school. When he graduated he had 2 extra credits just to avoid chunkin'.

No More Cotton

The weather factor made me stop growing cotton. It was just too cold. I sold my picker and sold my cattle herd and started growing double crop wheat and soy beans. The price was good for both, and the yield was good. I did good. I used three men and myself. We had 3 big tractors and one small one. We worked 1500 A beans and wheat. After we sold the cattle the men didn't have much to do in the winter time. All they did was repair the equipment. I did not have to be with them. They would do a good job if I were there or not.

Barney

I had 2 good bird dogs and a good labordore retreiver. I hunted quail until duck season started and then I hunted ducks. I had a black lab named Sharman. I also had a huge Irish Setter named Barny. Barny had radar in his brain. He would be in the pick up truck by the time the motor was started. If I went to town for parts and he was not in the truck when I was ready to go, I would leave him. He would come back to the parts place. If the truck was not there he would head for the farm. One hour later Barny would show up hot and thirsty.

He had a huge head and body. He was king dog in the erea. He did not have any time for other dogs. He could not stand for another dog to pee on his truck wheels. By the time another dog raised his leg Barny had him.

One day, I stopped at a neighbor's shop. He had a big dog with a bad rep. Barny was in the truck. The dog started barking and jumping up at Barny. Barny acted as though he wasn't watching him, the dog finely jumped up into Barny's truck. That was a big mistake. Barny had him flat of his back and had him by the throat before he knew what was going on. The dog's owner's name was Wm. Toots. I said Toots we had better get Barny loose from your dog. He said let him learn a lesson. I saw Barny get a new grip on the dogs throat. I jumped up into the truck and grabbed Barny by each ear and started twisting. Toots got his dog by his back legs and started pulling. Barny got to the point where he could not stand his ears being twisted and loosened his grip on the dog's throat. Toots pulled his dog out of the truck. He lay on the ground for a few minutes. He soon revived and got to his feet. He didn't look back. He did not want anymore trouble with Barny.

Barny thought he was a duck retreaver. We would have to lock him in a pen when we went duck hunting. He would swim across 200 A of open watter to get to where the duck blind was. He would stay there all day and shake from the cold watter. But everytime you killed ducks Barny would be back in the watter retreiving them. We had a propane stove he would get next to. I would cover him with a decoy sack. I have never seen a dog with so much desire to retreive, as he had. Cold watter did not bother Sharman and she did not want Barny to retreive any ducks. But if there was 2 ducks killed, Barny would always get one. It made my bones ake to see him shake. But it never made him sick.

In the early spring when the rivers would overflow the karp fish would go to the shaller watter to spawn. Barny loved to catch them. He did not care to eat them. He would carry them to high ground and drop them. There was a lady on the farm that liked to can them. She would clean them and put them in a can with salt watter and hot peper and put them in a pressure cooker for 30 minutes. She would fry them in patties and they were lotts like salmon. She called Barny her fishing dog. Each spring when the karp were running she would watch for Barny to start catching karp. She would get her bucketts and get the fish as Barny would drop them. Barny's only desire was to catch them. Some of the karp would weight 10-15 lbs, but most weighed 5-6 lbs.

We had cattle and you had to go through the pasture to get to the river bottom. Barny did not bother the cows as long as they were in the pasture. But if one was out in the soy bean field, Barny thought it was his job to get her back in the pasture. If he could not get it to the gate, he would make it jump the fence. After we got the soy beans harvested we would open the gates to the soy bean fields and let the cows get the beans we had left. It would run Barny crazy to see all the cows in the bean field. He would start rounding them up. He would not leave until all of the cows were back in the pasture.

Sharman

Sharman was a black female lab. She had no sense of direction. Barny would take her off hunting. He would always return without her. She would end up at some neighbor's house. They would call and we would go get her. I had a 2 year old granddaughter, Celia Jane, that Sharman was crazy about. She could crawl all over Sharman. When a stranger came to the house, Sharman did not want them to get close to the baby. You had to put Sharman in another room. If Sharman was in the yard with the baby, no stranger could come in the yard. I decided to test her one day. She was in the yard with the baby, I pulled my cap down over my face and started walking toward them. When I looked up, Sharman was just ready to attack. Laboadores are very protecative of their masters.

I have always said there was nothing like a good dog and a good woman and nothing worse than a mean dog and a mean woman. I have been blessed with a good woman for 60 years and I have had and still have some good dogs.

Duck Hunting

In my farming time, I always got up early. I always got to the resturent at 5 o'clock a.m. I always injoyed the fellowship. There was a general mixture of people. In the spring there would be lotts of people going fishing at Reelfoot Lake. And you would get all the fishing tales. There would be lotts of kidding and laughing. I have always thought there was no better medicine than a good laugh early in the morning.

During duck hunting season we cook breakfast at my hunting cabin. We cook country sausage most of the time. I had the largest banker in Tennessee as one of my hunting friends. He would sometimes bring a pork tenderloin. He was six foot two and weighed 300 lbs. He could consume a lotts eggs, t-loin biscuits and saw mill gravy. He also liked bull shot, a mixture of vodka and beef bullion. He would get his thermos hot and pour the bullshot into the thermos boiling hot. It would open up your sinus if the weather was real cold in a duck blind.

Most of the people on the farm liked to duck hunt. I had a 200 A plot set aside for them. If they didn't have a boat they would wade to their blind. One day the weather was 8 below freezing. We broke out a hole on the south side of the woods. We had a duck blind that would hold 8 people. The watter was froze everywhere but the South Fork River. The blind was close to the river. The ducks would fly the river for that was the only open water. When the ducks would see our decoys they would come strait in. It sounded like a war, when all the hunters would get their limit they would go back to the hunting cabin and a new group would come and take their place. We killed 123 ducks in that one blind that day.

My black lab Sharman would retreive the cripples on the ice, but there were times when there were so many cripples she could not retreive them all before they got away on the ice. One day the floor in the duck blind gave way and the big banker fell through. I thought he had lost his balls but he came out laughing. After 3 or 4 seasons the floors in duck blinds detorate and you have to replace them.

Since those days the ducks have gotten a lotts smarter. They will go to center of the fields to feed. You have to build your blind as low to the ground as possible. I have built blinds on styrophone. That way you can move it to any part of the field. It is better to pick up all your decoys each day. If you don't, the ducks will get used to seeing them and will not decoy to them. Ducks have all gotten a lott smarter in the past 50 years. Back then you could put out a spread of decoys and the ducks would pitch in on the first pass. Now they will circle out of range of your gun for 4 or 5 passes before they land on the outside of your decoys. Back then the pen tails, wegons, teal and blue bills would buzz your blocks, they don't do that any more.

T.W.R.A.

The Tennessee Wildlife Resources Agency is one of the largest land owners in Tennessee. They own land on all of the rivers in West Tenn. Some of the land they are doing nothing with. Thousands of acres are rented to local farmers to grow grain and row crops. They leave part of the grain for wild life and sell the rest. They are acquiring so much they cannot look after it all. They have land adjacent to my farm that they are doing nothing with. It is deep soil that has been deposited for 100 years, from the over flow of Pond Creek. I have offered to take my equipment and plant soy beans and wheat for wild life, but I have had no response from T.W.R.A. When I made the first offer this land was covered with small willows. If it had been planted in grain and soy beans as I suggested it would support wild life. It is now covered with large willows and no food for wild life can grow.

Some places the T.W.R.A. has done a good job, where they have rented the land to local farmers. I have seen a complete circle. When I was a boy in the 30's, the rivers were cleared and dredged and the hard wood did good. During the depression the W.P.A. was formed. It was a work project, paid for by the federal government. The W.P.A. cleared off the river banks and cleared the channel. As long as this was continued it worked fine and we had good drainage. But you will always have rains that the rivers cannot handle. This is especially so when the Mississippi is at flood stage.

Gambling on the Commodity Markets

During the President Nixon years, the farm commodity prices were real good. Some of my friends were making more money than they had ever made before. They were buying the most expensive machinery and equipment that was for sale. Before this time the highest price for soy beans was two-to-four dollers per bushell, and two dollers per bushell for wheat.

During the Nixon years the wheat price went to five dollers a bushell, and soy beans went to twelve dollars a bushell. The Lincoln and Codolack Dealers could not keep a car on their lots.

I had friends that were making more money than they had made in a life time, but they still weren't satisfied, they wanted to get it faster on the commodity board. The big dogs in Chicago let them make money for a short time. One of the largest traiders, a Memphis man, tried to corner the soy bean markett.

I was always afraid of the commodity markett. I had friends that were worth millions that lost every thing. One had ten thousand acres of land and lost it all. I had another that had eight thousand acres of land and a growing business and lost it all. It is really hard to see what stress it has placed their families in. I had one friend that got caught with the markett going down the limit for four days. You can't get out as long as the market is going down. He said he could not drink enough whiskey to put him to sleep.

Nixon was booted out as President and Ford took office. He put the first embargo on. It dropped the prices of soy beans and wheat and corn about one third. Later, the farm prices had just recovered when President Carter was elected. Interest rates went as high as 18 %. Most of the farmers in my erea had to borrow their opperating money. The price of wheat was five dollers and soy beans went to twelve dollars, so farmers were still able to make a proffit. President Carter put an embargo on for the second time, and before soy beans stopped going down they were five dollars. We had all of the storage on the farm full of soy beans, and ten thousand bushells stored at an elevator. It was a rough time but I had some surpless cash and we would not be put in too much of a bind.

Farmers have done fairly well for the last few years, but I don't feel too good about the future. I think the Freedom to Farm Bill that was passed in Congress may be the Freedom to Go Broke. Every thing the farmer has to buy has gone up. Every thing that he has to sell has gone down. Their used to be a floor under all commodities. You could not loose ever thing in one year. There is no floor, any more, that does not look good to me.

Early Settlers

When the first settler arrived in this part of West Tennessee, the land was all woods. The Indians did not spend much time here, they only used it as a hunting ground.

It is gently rolling. The first settler built his home on the highest hill. He was looking for a cool place in the summer, and to get away from the mosquito. The mosquito carried maleria. The summer time was called the Chill Season. At a certain time each day, you would have a high feever. You would start hot like you were burning inside and end up cold and shakeing. It would usually return about the same time each day. The reason for building on the highest hill, was the wind would help keep the mosquito blown away. The mosquito likes the low swampy places.

Most first settlers built near a spring so they would have watter all the year. They would find a big hollow log, they would burn and scrape the inside of the log. They would then dig the spring as deep as they could and place the log upright in the hole. They would burn a hole in the log, find a large cane, and insirt it in the hole. They would cut a peice of wood to fit over the log, this would keep animals snakes and frogs from getting in the watter and drowning. The watter would run freely out of the cane. They would cut a big block of wood and place it under the cane to set their watter buckett on, to ketch their watter. The watter ran freely all the time. To keep the excess watter from the spring, a long hollow cane would be inserted into the cane coming out of the log. This would run the excess watter away from the spring, and keep it from getting muddy around the spring.

The first settler cleared only small acres around their home. They let their stock run in the woods and fenced their crops, their hogs would eat acorns and other mast.

In 1818 their were just 18,000 people in West Tennessee, that was the year that the Chicasaw Indians sold this land to the goverment. By 1828 there was 100,000 settlers in this part of Tennessee. This migration mostly came by flat bottom boat. The Earth quake of 1811-1812 left the rivers cloged with huge trees. These people had to cut their way up the rivers to high land.

In the next ten years most of this country was cleared and put into row crops. Cotton was the largest cash crop grown. With this vast clearing and row cropping, the silt from erosion started to fill the creeks and rivers.

After the Civil War most of the land was worked by the share system. The land owner would furnish everything but the labor. He furnished the seed, fertlizer, all the tools and animals needed to make the crop. He also furnished the share cropper a house. The cropper got half the price of the crop for his labor.

There was also a tenant farmer. The owner furnished him a house but the tenant farmers owned all of his equipment and furnished every thing. He raised and gathered all of the crops, and paid the land owner one third of the crop. If their was any fertilizer used on the land owner paid for one third.

Rivers Silting Up

By the early 1900's all of the rivers flowing into the Mississippi had began to fill with silt. Gullies began to form on the higher hills. This was highly erodible soil, and a lotts should never been cleared.

In 1915 a drainage districk was formed. It included Obion and Forked Deer Rivers. These rivers drained all of north west Tennessee into the Mississippi River. The land owners voted to assess a drainage tax on the land drained by these rivers. The drainage districk hired a dredge boat to dig the new channell. Where the dredge cut through the old river, the upper end of the old river was closed off. The lower end remained open so the watter could drain into the new channell.

This system worked well for several years. The wooded land drained and the timber grew. If the new river channell had been maintained and the river channell snogged each year, the system would have worked, but for manny years nothing was done to the new channell.

The trees grew on both sides of the river banks. The trees were watter maples, cotton wood, watter oak, and watter birch. These trees were fast growing and within 20 years there were large trees growing on both side of the river. In the winter you would have ice storms, and the trees on the banks would slide into the rivers. The soil on the banks was verry alluviaol and would not hold the trees in the ice storm. Huge drifts would form in the rivers. Some were two and three miles long. This caused the river to overflow in the summer time and kill some of the hardwood timber in the low land. It got to the point that all the low land was flooded to the edge of the hills.

PART IV

FARMING THE BOTTOMLAND
By
Jack and Celia Hudson

Earthquake

In December 1811 a tremendous earthquake occurred in the vicinity of what is now the bootheel of Missouri. It is thought to have been 8.6 on the Richter scale. At least two of the aftershocks are thought to have been 8.6. The next day another earthquake occurred in the same vicinity.

At that time, commercial trade was carried on by flat boats on the Ohio and upper Mississippi River. Flatboats were built out of sawed lumber. Cotton and livestock, hogs and pork were some of the main staples carried by the flatboats to New Orleans. There they unloaded and sold their goods. Then they took the flatboats apart and sold the lumber. Then they would make their way to Natchez, Mississippi and follow the Natchez Trace to Nashville. Several flatboats were backed up when another great earthquake occurred. Most of the boats were lost, but some were anchored at New Madrid and survived.

In January 1812 another big earthquake caused huge sand boils in Tennessee and created a dam across Reelfoot Creek. This was the beginning of Reelfoot Lake.

In February came of the largest quake of all. It caused the Mississippi River to run backwards between Island #9 and Island #10. It caused such towering waves of water to be thrown over the banks that thousands of acres of trees were shattered into splinters and stumps near Island #8.

East of the Mississippi River below Reelfoot Lake were huge bluffs, some as high as 300 feet or more. From 1811-1812 til the early 1900's people deserted these lands.

Clearing the Bottomlands

Mengle Box and Basket Company acquired deeds to most of this land probably from land grants to the soldiers of the Revolutionary War.

Mengle Box Co. built their mill at present day Menglewood. They built spur tracks in all directions and used a small locomotive to haul their logs back to the mill. All of these were cut by two men using a crosscut saw. The logs were snaked to the railroad by mules and oxen.

After Menglewood finished logging all of their land they sold it for a dollar an acre. Most of this land was left in woods.

A family would buy and try to clear 50 acres. A house would be built on 15 foot poles to stay above the Mississippi River floods.

A few acres would be cleared each year. Trees were circled by an axe so that they would die and the limbs would fall off.

Farming had to be done around the stumps. It would take several years to clear 50 acres. The fallen limbs would be piled around the trees and set on fire.

The drinking water came from a driven pump, which usually ran 20 feet deep. The water always had an oily skim or an awful smell.

The houses had no screens to keep the mosquitoes out. At night a fire would be built where the smoke would blow back through the house and run the mosquitoes off. All of the family would have malaria in the summer. They would work the fields until noon and them come in and take their dose of quinine.

Chickens would be kept in a pen under the house at night to keep them safe from varmints. Most families had eight or ten children. Not all of them lived to adulthood. A lot of them died in infancy. There were no doctors within less than twenty miles.

In Menglewood land and all of the land from the bluffs to the Mississippi River were still in small farms in 1947. After that the woodlands were sold for $10 an acre.

I had a friend who bought several thousand acres of timberland. He had ten of the largest clearing machines. He would clear the land and rent it to other farmers to work on shares.

The land was very rich and made huge soybean yields. This was when soybeans were getting in full swing. This friend would clear four to five hundred acres a year. He ended up with about 10,000 acres of land.

There were several other people buying and clearing land. There were people who owned machines and did custom work. The land that I cleared was done by custom clearing at so much an hour. In ten years all of the land from the bluffs to the Mississippi River had been cleared.

Now, from the bluff to the Mississippi River, all of the houses have been torn down and the land is in huge tracts. It made me sad about all the hard labor that had gone into those small farms.

The land that I cleared was done by pushing the trees into long wind rows. They would be set on fire. The dozier would keep pushing the trees into the fire until most of the logs were burned. We would then run a huge disc over the land. Then we would drill the beans and run a huge roller over the ground to push the chunks back in the ground. This would keep the chunks out of the combine while we were combining beans.

The next year we would take a chisel plow and move all the plows to the back of the chisel plow and use this as a rake. We would rake the chunks up in huge piles. Either we would haul the chunks out of the field or take a backhoe and bury them. It would take about five years to remove all the chunks from the ground.

Going to Town with a Load of Cotton

The mother and the smaller children would stay at home. Those six years and older would make the trip to town. The mother had begun preparations the day before. The children took the wash tub to the pump and filled it. Each one would take his bath with homemade lye soap. Mother would tell each one to be sure to get all the gumbo from between their toes. If there happened to be a scratch the lye soap would burn like fire. The older children would bathe the younger ones.

The next morning they would get up before dawn and eat breakfast. Each one put on clean clothes, usually overalls and a shirt. After breakfast the father would hook the mules to the wagon, being sure to tie the lantern on the coupling pole, so that a car would be able to see the wagon.

The kids would take 2 quilts and tie over the cotton to keep from knocking the cotton off the wagon. The quilt would be to sleep on coming home. The mother would fix country ham and biscuits, putting them in a shoe box for food on the way to town (two boxes so one would be left for lunch.) They would crawl on the wagon. The younger ones would go back to sleep.

If they had to go to the bathroom, an older one would help the younger ones. The wagon never stopped, so the older one hurried the younger ones saying it would be a long way to catch the wagon.

There was a cross road called Big Boy Junction. The older ones would tell the younger ones they had better go before they got to Big Boy Junction. There would be houses there and no place to go to the bathroom. It would take about an hour from there to town.

Just as you came into town there was a gin, "The Farmers Union Gin." There were huge trees all around the lot. They would park under a tree and spread a quilt on the ground.

The father would take the cotton to the gin and have it ginned off the wagon. Then he would get his check and bring the wagon and mules back to the tree and loosen the mules from the wagon. He would put corn in the feed box and tie the mules to the tree. He would remove the bridles so the mules could eat. He would tie the ropes to the halter.

There was a small store across the road where they got cold drinks. He would take them to get their drinks and bring back to the wagon. They would eat country ham and biscuits and drink their cold drinks. Most of the time a big R.C.

It was one mile from there to town. They would all line up and walk to town on the sidewalk. Each one would get a dime so he could go to the Bloody Bucket to see a movie. After the show they would walk back to the gin and begin their journey back home. The father would give them a treat. He would go across to the store and buy a stick of baloney and a loaf of bread and get another drink.

He would hitch up the mules for the trip back home. They would get in the wagon. The father would slice the baloney and they would have their baloney and drink on the way home. They would get 2/3 of the way home before it began to get dark. Then they would light the lantern and tie it to the back tailgate.

The road was a one-way concrete slab that ran from the river to town. If you met any traffic you had to get off the slab because people coming to town had the right of way. After dark the owls hooted and the bob cats squalled and no one wanted to go to the bathroom because no one wanted to catch the wagon in the dark.

When they got home all tried to talk at once and tell the little ones what they saw and did in town. It was their biggest day of the year.

The mother would make sure they brought the quilts in because some of them had to sleep on them.

Cotton Picking

The schools were closed the months of Sept. and Oct. for cotton picking. A wagon would be placed in the middle of the cotton field. Each picker had his own sack (small ones for the younger ones and large ones for the older ones). The younger ones picked on the same row as the older ones. The older ones made sure there was no cotton left on the stalks.

When the sacks were filled they took them to the wagon where the cotton was weighed and emptied in the wagon. The weight would be tallied each night so that they would know when they had a bale of cotton.

The next day they picked until they had enough to make a bale. A bale was usually about 500 lbs. of lint cotton. It would take 1500 lbs. of seed cotton to gin out 500 lbs. of lint.

Each family had about 15 acres of cotton. It would take about 30 days to pick it and usually made 15 bales.

Pecans—The Second Cash Crop

The second cash crop was pecans. The Menglewood Co. did not cut pecan or hickory trees. This lumber did not suit their purposes. The Lee family would take their wagons and go into the woods following the logging road. They would go from pecan tree to pecan tree. They would remove all the fallen limbs under the pecan trees and place a tarpaulin on the ground. One of the older boys had climbing spikes. He would climb the tree and hook a rope around the tree trunk. The rope was a huge one about 50 ft. long that was used by the tow boats to tie the barges up during high water. The mules were loosened from the wagon and hooked to the rope. The mules would come to the end of the rope with a jerk and shake the pecans down. One person on each corner of the tarpaulin would raise it and force the pecans to the center. They would pick up the pecans and sack them. Then they would spread the tarpaulin out and repeat the same process. With this process pecans could be harvested much quicker. Most people would pick up pecans, which had fallen from the trees. It was a slow process. The Lee Family with their process got a head start on everyone else. Most of the farmers waited until they had picked their cotton and gathered their corn to start picking up pecans. The Bob Lee family started picking up pecans before gathering their corn. That gave them a head start on the other pecan gatherers.

By the last of November, the Lee family had picked up 2,000 lbs. of pecans and had them stacked under their house.

Mr. Lee went to town and went by the pecan buyers. When he came back home there was a man with a truck parked in front of his house. The man was from Illinois and had come down to buy pecans. Old man Lee told him that he had 2,000 lbs. of pecans stacked under his house, and asked what he would pay per pound for the whole lot. The man from Illinois offered him twice as much as he could get from the local buyers. Old man Lee said, "Man, you have bought your self some pecans, but I have to have cash on the barrel head." The man from Illinois backed his truck up to the house and set his scales on the ground. All of the Lee family started moving the pecans.

Rosie the oldest child was good at arithmetic. Her father said, "Rosie you set right here by these scales and put down how much each sack weighs." The man from up north would open each sack so he was sure they were pecans. He had some experience with people putting bricks in with the pecans. After he had emptied and checked several sacks, he decided that Mr. Lee was honest. He weighed the rest of them and stacked them in his truck.

When all of the sacks had been weighed and the amounts tallied, the man from up North reached under the seat of his truck and pulled out a huge sack of money. He counted out $1,264. The Lee family had never seen that much money in their lives. The next day old man Lee and his 2 oldest boys went to town. The Ford car dealer had a Model A Ford truck with a cab. He wanted $500 for it. Old man Lee said, "I'll give you $450 cash on the barrel head for it." The car dealer took off his cap and scratched his head, walked around the truck. He said, "Man you have bought yourself a truck." Joe, the oldest boy could drive, so they drove to the bank and old man Lee put the rest of the money in the bank. It was the biggest amount of money he ever had in his life. When he got back home the little Lees crawled over and under every inch of the truck.

Corn

Mr. Lee had 100 acres of corn. It was Neil Paymaster, a white corn with very large ears. The land was real rich and the corn was good. He had spaced the stalks of corn about three feet apart. He had beans and peas planted in the spaces between the stalks.

One night someone knocked on his door. When he opened the door there stood the Tucker brothers. They said, "Mr. Bob, we're here to try to buy your corn."

The Tucker brothers owned a farm on the highest bluff. Coon Creek ran through part of it. They had a small building on Coon Creek. There was a little valley where Coon Creek went over a small waterfall. They had their moonshine whiskey still set up there. They had a huge copper cooker. It would hold a barrel of mash. They would put fifty pounds of sugar to a barrel of corn meal. They would add yeast and other ingredients and water that were needed to make the mash start working. Then they would cover the mash barrels with a heavy cover to keep out the raccoons and other varmints.

The Tucker brothers had a very neat operation and it was very clean for the times. They would cook the mash and the steam would go into the copper worm [tubing] and come out the other end of the worm as condensed alcohol. The worm would be placed under the waterfall. The cold water would condense the steam and the liquid would run from the worm into a container. It would run into the container for the whiskey. The first run of the mash would end up 150 proof alcohol.

The brothers would cut the first run with one half spring water. This made it about 80 proof alcohol. Then they would put the water in the mash and cook it one more time. The second run would usually be about 80 proof alcohol.

After they had cooked it the second time they would take the mash out of the cooker and put it in a barrel and take it down to the hog pen. The mash would be fed to the hogs. It was really funny to watch the hogs. After eating the mash they would wobble around and squeal like some people on a happy drunk. This mash would really fatten the hogs.

The Tucker brothers said, "Mr. Lee, we know you have some very good corn. We will give you twice what you can get anywhere else. But this is what you'll have to do. You will have to shuck each ear and shell off the end of each ear to get rid of all the faulty grain. Then you will have to haul the corn to Miss Monroe's flour mill. There she will shell the corn and grind the kernels into corn meal. You will bring the meal back to your home and put it under the house. We will pay you for the shelling and grinding of the corn. Miss Monroe will weigh the ears of corn and we will pay you twice the going price of corn."

Mr. Lee put all of his kids in the field gathering corn. When they had gathered a wagonload they would bring it to the house. At the house they would shuck the corn and shell off the ends to get rid of the faulty grain. Then the ears of corn would be thrown into the truck. They shelled corn in wash tubs. When the tub was full, they would pour the corn into sacks and put it under the house for hog feed during the winter. This type of corn was not good for horses, mules and cattle. But it was good for hog feed.

Going to Church

In the mid nineteen thirties the economy was still very bad. People had to scratch and scrape to make ends meet. Those who lived on the farm and had cows, hogs and chickens, ate very well. They would pick black berries for jam and jelly, and wild plums for preserves.

From Mr. Lee's home it was about four miles to their church on the Mississippi River. They would hitch the mules to the wagon and the whole family would get in for the ride to church. The church was built on poles just like all of the houses. The circuit rider preacher came once a month. He was usually a young seminary pupil from Lambuth College in Jackson.

There was a permanent dinner table built from post to post under the church. There was a barrel seat on each side of the table for the people to sit on. The women would usually fry country ham and make biscuits. Food had to be some things that would not spoil because there was no refrigeration. Cakes and pies were always part of the meal.

The preacher would always pick up a 50 lb. block of ice at the icehouse. He would bring it to the church and place it in a 55-gallon barrel. The women would bring prepared tea and pour it over the ice so they could have iced tea with their dinner.

The church service would begin at nine o'clock and usually last until eleven. This allowed time for the meal to be cooked and ready for eating.

The church had a huge wash kettle. They used it to cook the wild game that the man had killed early in the morning. They would fill the kettle about half full of water, and then put about two cups of salt and a dozen red peppers in the kettle. They would add the squirrels, usually 30 to 40, to the kettle and cover the kettle and cook them about two hours. Then vegetables, such as potatoes, onion, carrots and a dozen tomatoes would be added and cooked until done. When there was corn in the roasting ear stage they would be added to the stew.

When the sermon was over everyone would gather under the church for the meal. Each family had brought their own eating utensils—usually a tin plate, a knife, fork and spoon—for its use. The preacher would say the blessing and then they would line up at the stew pot where someone help their plates.

After everyone had finished eating and the stew pot had been cleaned with boiling water and lye soap they would get a hymnal for the singing. Two plates would be passed around for an offering to pay the preacher. The preacher did not expect a lot because they had little to give. But they did bring other things for the preacher such as jams, jellies and occasionally a country ham.

They would sing the familiar songs such as "The Old Rugged Cross" and "In the Garden." After about an hour of singing everyone would gather their utensils and the remnants of cakes and pies, if any were left. Then they would load in their wagons and start home.

When they arrived home from church Mr. Lee decided to check his cornfield. He and the children had picked all the beans and peas that he had planted in the corn. He had turned his cow and hogs into the cornfield to eat the remains of the beans and peas and corn stalks.

When he got in the cornfield he saw he had about 100 extra cows and 50 extra hogs. He said, "Oh my God, the old son-a-bitch has done it again." He went back to the house and got his boys and they gathered their shot guns. They got on their horses and rounded up the cows and hogs and got them started back toward Menglewood. They started shooting the cows in the rear ends to discourage them from returning.

The 1937 Floods

The U.S. Engineers had warned the people along the flood plain that there was a possibility that one of the largest floods along the Mississippi River in several years was imminent.

Mr. Lee had been seeing a certain empty house on top of the bluff. It was a house that had not been lived in for three or four years. Ben Smith had owned the house and 200 acres of land. The land was all hills and hollows and woods except for 40 acres, which had been cleared along Coon Creek. Ben Smith had the land paid for and he had $10,000 in the People's Bank. This was money he had collected from the government upon the death of one of his sons during the First World War. When he received the death notice the only information was "missing in action." He and his wife decided to put the money in the bank and not spend any of it, hoping that some day their son might return. Mr. Smith had already given his daughter $1,000 to buy a farm with two houses on it.

He and his wife decided to build a new house and to borrow the money for house from the Equitable Life Insurance Company.

By 1932 most of the banks were closing their doors and declaring bankruptcy. Mr. Smith was left without any money. He and his wife stayed on in the house for two years. They could not pay interest on the debt, so the Equitable Life Insurance Company forced them to move. They moved into an extra house on their daughter's farm.

Mr. Lee called the Equitable Life Insurance agent and asked him how much they wanted for the farm. The agent said he would sell the farm and house for $2,000. Mr. Lee was to pay $1,000 at purchase and $250 a year for four years at six percent interest. Mr. Lee went to the insurance office and gave the agent a check for $1,000 and received the deed to the farm. After having the deed recorded, he went home and gathered his wife and children and took them to the house to begin cleaning in and around the house, which had been vacant for 2 years.

When he went home to get his family he looked at his flood gauge and saw the water had risen one foot that day. He and the boys began loading the livestock, hogs and chickens and moved them to the new house. The water was rising so fast he had to drive the mules and cows through the water. They had to go back to the house and load the corn. After unloading the corn at the new house they had to rush back to the old house to get the furniture and their clothes. The backwater had risen so fast the truck barely got through. They worked all night getting settled in.

The next morning they drove to the edge of the backwater and found it had risen 4 feet that night. There would be no more access to the old house except by boat.

People were beginning to arrive at the bluff to escape the backwater. Some escaped with only the clothes on their backs.

Mr. Lee and his boys decided to build a boat. They got in the truck and drove to the Tucker brother's home. He told them that he wanted to buy some lumber to build a boat. The Tuckers told him that he had a stack of lumber behind the house. They were welcome to get all the lumber they wanted and there would be no charge.

Mr. Lee told them that all his tools were in his house in the backwater. The Tuckers brought their tools and helped them build the boat. It was about 6 feet wide and 14 feet long. When they finished it they wondered how they were going to get the boat to the backwater.

So the Tuckers hitched a team of their mules to their wagon and they all loaded the boat on the wagon and took it down to the backwater and unloaded it into the water. The boat had to sit in the water overnight so the lumber would swell and stop the leaks.

Everybody in the area was looking for a boat. The Lees knew they had to have someone there to watch the boat to keep it from being stolen. The Tuckers said they would stay with the boat until the Lees could go to their new home and return.

The oldest Lee boy ate his supper and put on the warmest clothes he had. He brought an axe and some wood to build a fire to keep him warm during the night. The rest of the Lee family worked most of the night fixing a place for the animals and arranging their furniture. Mrs. Lee said a prayer of thanks for her new house and a safe place from the backwater.

At daylight the next morning one of the Tuckers came down to relieve the Lee boy so he could go home, eat his breakfast and get his father and brothers back to the boat. The Lees had made them two long paddles and an oarlock for each side of the boat. When they arrived at the boat it was half full of water. They had a five-gallon bucket to dip the water out. After they had dipped the water out they pulled the boat up on dry land. They took the hammers and drove the nails down on all of the joints. Then they cut poles to put under the boat to roll it back into the water.

The water had risen five feet during the night. They knew they had a hard pull to get the boat back to the house. They rolled the boat down to the road that went from the bluff to the river. The water was half way up the tall trees. They started paddling down the road. In places the current was so swift that it would put the boat into the trees. They would have to pull the boat from branch to branch until they reached the current. Then they would get back in the road and be able to row again. The water was so deep that a pole would not push the boat.

They reached the house after about three and a half hours of rowing. They were all exhausted. They tied the boat to the top porch. They knew that the water was over twenty feet deep at the house. They went into the house and placed some planks on top of some barrels. Then they placed some things they thought they could salvage on the boards. That would give them four more feet.

Then they rowed across to the barn. The water had already covered the mount that the barn was built on. They saw there was nothing they could do about the corn since the water was up to the edge of it.

They decided that the best thing for them to do was to get the boat back to dry land as soon as possible. The trip back was just as hard. They had to pull the boat from limb to limb until they crossed the swift current. It was almost sundown when they reached dry land. They were all exhausted.

There were people who had made it all the way from the Mississippi River. They said they had never seen the Mississippi River rise that fast before. They had seen three houses go down the river that day. That day people were seen on top of their houses. There were people on ferryboats trying to rescue those in trouble. They told the ferry boat captain where they had seen people on top of houses.

The Lees paddled their boat back to the place they had left it the night before. They knew they could not make the trip back to the house again. They felt lucky to have made the trip because it was a very dangerous undertaking. Then they got in their truck and drove to their new home.

The next morning they got in their car and drove back to the boat landing. They found that the river had risen four more feet during the night. They knew that everything in the house and barn would be ruined. They thought they would never see the house again because it would be washed away.

At the boat landing there were a hundred desperate people from the backwater. They had lost everything.

Mr. Lee decided that the best thing he could do was to take these people to town so they could find a place to stay and something to eat. He took the first load of people to the old cigar factory building in Dyersburg. The factory was not operating and the building was empty.

The building was half full of flood victims when they arrived. The churches of the town had set up a food kitchen to feed the refugees. The National Guard had brought bales of blankets and cots to the building for the flood victims to sleep on. Mr. Lee unloaded the people and went back for more of the flood victims. He continued to do this all day.

He went home that night and when he came back the next morning there were just as many flood victims there as the day before. He hauled victims all that day. It was so pathetic to see these poor people who had such a hard life and to know what few possessions that they had accumulated had washed away with the flood. The churches asked for donations of clothing and shoes and especially coats. The flood victims were glad to get anything. For some of them the only clothes they had were what they had on their backs.

Miss Lucy Hart was the head of the Red Cross for Dyer County. She went around to the collection points in the county to pick up donations for the flood victims.

The churches would serve two meals a day—breakfast and another meal at about two o'clock. The dairies in the community contributed milk and K.W. Rogers Company contributed a lot of groceries.

All the flood victims could think of was all the mud and slime that would have to be cleaned up at their homes. Most of them did not even know whether they would have a house to go back to and some of them would not.

Mrs. Lee was really happy to know that she would not have to go back to the house on stilts and the backwater. The TVA had just run a line in front of their house. They were able to connect to the line, so Mr. Lee bought a new refrigerator and washing machine. Some morning when Mrs. Lee awoke she would wonder if she had died and gone to heaven.

When the flood receded to the point that you could drive from the bluff to the river, Mr. Lee and his two sons drove back to the house on the stilts. They were surprised to see it still standing.

Everything in the house was ruined except two barrels of corn they had saved for the hogs. All of the corn in the barn was ruined. All of the pea seeds and bean seeds were gone.

Mr. Lee said, "I'll not plant any more beans and peas in the corn. When I gather the corn I will set the fields on fire and burn the stalks. He can turn all of his livestock loose and it won't bother me anymore."

Free River Press
Folk Literature Series

Heartland Series
Heartland Portrait
Voices from the Land
More Voices from the Land
Simple Times
Independence, Iowa
Clermont, Iowa
Village Voices

Outsider Series
Five Street Poets
Passing Thru
Lion's Share
Hitchhiker's Dream
From within Walls
Let Me Tell You Where I Used to Live

Mississippi Delta Series
Dirt and Duty
Fishin', Fightin', Feedin' & Farmin'

Sixties Series
A Rogues Island Memoir